Contents

To the Teacher

To many elementary teachers, social studies is the "dessert" of their teaching day: a subject that allows for interactive lessons and hands-on activities. It is also a subject for which there is usually little time in the course of the school day. Many teachers nevertheless find ways to incorporate projects, activities, simulations, and other performance activities into the classroom, to "bring social studies alive" for their students.

Activities in *Houghton Mifflin Social Studies*

Numerous sources exist for projects and activities, but the challenge for most teachers is to find options that are manageable, flexible, and support the required curriculum. *Houghton Mifflin Social Studies* addresses these concerns with activities that are

- **Realistic** Program activities use easy-to-find materials and span time blocks that can be easily scheduled.

- **Optional** Activities and projects engage and motivate students, yet are not required to cover the curriculum.

- **Based on tested objectives** Activities and projects are focused on required content and skills and use a hands-on, interactive approach to helping students learn the material they need to know.

These activities and projects are found in the following program components:

Student Book

- Hands-on and writing activities in each Lesson Review support different learning modalities and writing modes.

- Extend Lesson activities are leveled for extra support or challenge opportunities.

- Chapter Review activities synthesize important concepts of the chapter.

- Unit Reviews include opportunity for hands-on review and a Current Events project tied to information on the Web from Weekly Reader.

Bringing Social Studies Alive

Use with *United States History*

Teacher's Edition

- Activities and projects in the Student Book are supported by scoring rubrics.

- Every unit begins with leveled and cross-curricular activities.

- Support for every Core Lesson includes activity suggestions for differentiated instruction and cross-curricular links.

- Extend Lesson support includes suggestions for activities for differentiated instruction and cross-curricular links.

Activities in *Bringing Social Studies Alive* cover the strands of social studies: Citizenship, Culture, Economics, Geography, and History. The Unit Planner notes the instructional approaches used for each activity and gives estimates of the time needed to complete it. For each unit you will find these opportunities:

- **Long-term Project** A unit project develops over the course of the unit. Students synthesize large concepts and develop their writing, research, and presentation skills. In-depth support is provided.

- **Hands-on Activities** These are engaging, short-term activities.

- **Geography Activities** Map and globe skills and geography concepts further geographic literacy.

- **Performance Activities** Included are citizenship simulations, Readers' Theater, and other speaking and listening opportunities.

Bringing Social Studies Alive also features a special section of **Personal Finance Activities**. These activities develop economic understanding through the personal finance skills students will need throughout their lives.

- Banking
- Budgeting
- Investing

Unit Planner

Long-Term Project Pages 2–3	Materials Needed

American Indian Dioramas
 	
Students research American Indian nations and build dioramas depicting the ways they lived.
 	
Time Needed: 4 weeks **Strand:** Geography
 	
Lesson Link: Chapter 2, Lessons 2, 3, 4, and 5
	• boxes • craft sticks
	• construction • art supplies as
	  paper needed:
	• cloth and crayons, paint,
	  leather scraps glue, and
	• foil markers

Geography Activities Pages 4–5	
Activity 1 Lots of Water . . . Can You Drink It? Students learn about Earth's water using grid paper, maps, and graphs. **Time Needed:** 30–40 minutes **Strand:** Geography **Lesson Link:** Chapter 1, Lesson 2	• outline map of the world • $\frac{1}{4}$" or centimeter grid paper • colored pencils or markers
Activity 2 Many Regions, One Map Students make a single map to show where many different American Indian nations lived. **Time Needed:** 30–40 minutes **Strand:** Geography **Lesson Link:** Chapter 2, Lessons 2, 3, 4, and 5	• outline map of North America • colored pencils or markers

Hands-On Activities Pages 6–7	
Activity 1 Make a Model of an Artifact Students research an American Indian nation and make an artifact representing its culture. **Time Needed:** 30–40 minutes **Strand:** Culture **Lesson Link:** Chapter 2, Lessons 1, 2, 3, 4, and 5	• markers, and • paper, foil crayons scraps, • modeling clay cardboard • scissors tubes • glue
Activity 2 Build an Ancient Pueblo Village Model Students research and build a model of an Ancient Pueblo village. **Time Needed:** 30–40 minutes **Strand:** History **Lesson Link:** Chapter 2, Lesson 1	• paint, crayons • empty milk • modeling clay cartons, or • construction small boxes paper • heavy string • scissors, glue • craft sticks

Performance Activity Pages 8–11	
Access Archaeology Students put on a play about archaeologists discussing when the first people may have arrived in the Americas. **Time Needed:** 30–40 minutes **Strand:** History **Lesson Link:** Chapter 2, Lesson 1	none
For Personal Finance, see pp. 108–119.	

American Indian Dioramas

Introduction

The lives of each of the American Indian nations mentioned in the text—Pacific Northwest, Southwest, Great Plains, and Eastern Woodlands—were shaped by their physical environment. As a result, each nation's quest for food and shelter was markedly different from the others. Students can create dioramas presenting the prevailing conditions for each American Indian culture.

MATERIALS

- shoe boxes
- construction paper
- cloth and leather scraps
- foil
- craft sticks
- art supplies as needed: crayons, paint, glue, and markers

Project Plan
Week 1: Choose a Group to Research 30–45 minutes

Open a class discussion, pointing out that the natural resources, landforms, and climate of the different regions influenced the lives of the American Indians. Use these questions to highlight the differences between the regions.

- *What did the the Northwest Indians use to build shelters?*
- *How was it different from the materials used by the Southwest Indians?*
- *Why did Western Plains Indians construct houses that were easily moveable while Eastern Plains Indians built permanent lodges?*

Indicate to students that they can show the differences in each nation's way of life by constructing a distinct diorama for each nation.

Direct students to form groups of four. Have each group choose an American Indian nation—Tlingit, Hopi, Comanche, Haudenosaunee—to research and represent. Encourage students to list and/or sketch the items they wish to include in their dioramas. Remind groups that the dioramas should show how the people lived, including representations of food and shelter.

Week 2: Decide What to Show 30–45 minutes

Tell groups to decide whether they want to show how shelter was built or how people lived in the shelter. In the same way, encourage groups to decide if they will show how food was obtained or how it was prepared and eaten. Interested groups may want to show how related families interacted and what kind of government united families in the nation. Students should gather the supplies they will need based on their decisions.

Week 3: Construct Dioramas 30–60 minutes

Direct students to construct their dioramas. As dioramas near completion, tell groups that each diorama will need a title and a written description that will help viewers understand what the diorama shows. Each group may wish to choose one student to present the diorama. This student can develop a presentation script based on the diorama's written description.

Week 4: Describe the Scene 30–45 minutes

Display the dioramas around the classroom for viewing. Allow time for students to study the dioramas in detail. Then invite a representative of each group to describe the scene to the entire class.
If feasible, moderate a question-and-answer session for each diorama.

Name _____ Date _____

 # Lots of Water . . . Can You Drink It?

You already know that water is an important resource that humans have. In this activity, use grid paper and maps and make a graph to learn about Earth's water.

MATERIALS

- Outline map of the world
- $\frac{1}{4}$" or centimeter grid paper
- colored pencils or markers

Compare Land and Water

1. First, use grid paper to find out about how much of Earth's surface is covered with water. Place a sheet of grid paper over or under the world outline map. Carefully trace around the world's land masses, both continents and islands. Do not include Antartica in this activity.

2. Lightly shade the land masses.

3. Compare the area covered by water to the area covered by land masses. Try counting the number of squares on the land masses and the number of squares on the water. Estimate how much of Earth's surface is covered by water by using a fraction, such as $\frac{1}{4}$, $\frac{1}{3}$, $\frac{1}{2}$, $\frac{2}{3}$, or $\frac{3}{4}$.

Make a Bar Graph

Your comparison may lead you to believe that Earth has water to spare. Most of Earth's water is ocean water. It is salty and cannot be used to drink or to water crops. Make a bar graph to show how much water is really available for human use.

Use the information in the table below to make a bar graph on grid paper. The graph should show the amount of ocean water and fresh water available. Be sure to label each part of the graph.

Water Source	Percent
Ocean water	97.2
Fresh water (glaciers, ice caps, ground water, lakes, rivers)	2.8
Total Water	100.0

Write one or two sentences telling what conclusion you can draw from your graph.

Many Regions, One Map

In this unit, you learned about the ancient Americans and other North American Indian nations and where they lived. In this activity, you will make a single map that shows where several different American Indian nations lived.

MATERIALS
- outline map of North America
- colored pencils or markers

1. On the outline map, make a legend using a different color or pattern for each of the following American Indian nations. Be sure that you can easily tell the ancient American cultures from the later American Indian nations.

   - Adena and Hopewell
   - Ancient Pueblo
   - Aztecs
   - Tlingit
   - Hopi
   - Comanche
   - Haudenosaunee

2. Use the colors and patterns in your legend to show on the outline map where each nation lived. Reread the page about these groups in chapter 2. You also may need to refer to maps in the Atlas at the back of your textbook.

3. Use your map to write a short paragraph describing which American Indian nations might easily have traded with one another.

Name _____ Date _____

HANDS ON   ACTIVITY

 # Make a Model of an Artifact

Introduction

What could people learn about you if they looked at the objects in your home? You know that one way we learn about people who lived long ago is by studying artifacts, which are objects made by people of the past. Some of the artifacts that help us learn about the American Indian nations are arrowheads, pots, and beads. You can make a model of an American Indian artifact.

MATERIALS

- markers and crayons
- modeling clay
- scissors
- glue
- paper, foil scraps, cardboard tubes

Getting Started

- Choose one of the American Indian nations presented in your textbook.

- Reread the description of the nation. Pay particular attention to descriptions of any artifacts. You may want to look for additional pictures of artifacts in reference books or an encyclopedia.

- Make a short list of the kinds of artifacts that helped people learn about your chosen American Indian nation. Choose an artifact you find interesting.

- Make a model of the artifact using art materials. For example, you can use clay to make a small pot or bits of fabric to make miniture clothing.

Checklist

☐ **1.** My model is similar to artifacts made by _____, the American Indian nation I chose.

☐ **2.** My model tells something about how the people traveled, what clothes they wore, their history, how they prepared the foods they ate, or what tools they made.

Name _____ Date _____

Build an Ancient Pueblo Village Model

Introduction

What materials were used to build your home? Maybe the building is made of wood or bricks. Chapter 2 describes the houses built by the Ancient Pueblo, an American Indian civilization that lived in the American Southwest. Study the picture of Ancient Pueblo housing shown on page 42 of your textbook. You can build a model of an Ancient Pueblo village using the picture as a reference.

MATERIALS

- paint, crayons
- modeling clay
- construction paper
- scissors, glue
- empty small and large milk cartons, small boxes
- heavy string, craft sticks

Getting Started

- Reread the description of the Ancient Pueblo housing in your textbook. Be sure you understand how the people used ladders to connect one story of a building with another. If you have time, look for additional pictures of Ancient Pueblo housing in reference books or an encyclopedia.

- Make a list of the details of the housing. For example, what material did the Ancient Pueblo use for walls? Did the homes have windows? Was part of the building in a cave or built into the side of a rocky cliff?

Checklist

☐ 1. My model Ancient Pueblo buildings are similar to buildings shown on page 42.

☐ 2. My model shows how the people moved from one building to another and from one story to another.

☐ 3. My model shows how the houses could be built into the side of a cliff.

Access Archaeology

For years, scientists believed the first people arrived in the Americas by traveling across Beringia. Some believed that they arrived between 10,000 and 27,000 years ago. Others think they may have arrived earlier or later. No one knows for sure. However, archaeologists working in the southeastern United States have found clues that are prompting scientists to rethink some of their ideas.

Cast of Characters

Jon Brooks:	"Access Archaeology" Host
Professor Marge Sunamoto:	Professor of Archaeology
Jack Williams:	Field Reporter
Dr. Robert White:	Leader of an excavation in Virginia
Miwa Huang:	Remote Reporter
Martin Majors:	leader of an excavation in South Carolina
Aimee Hazelton:	Dig Volunteer #1
Rashid Tikrit:	Dig Volunteer #2
Ahman DeSango:	Dig Volunteer #3

Scene 1: A newsroom conference table

Jon Brooks: Good morning. Today, we're talking with a leading professor of archaeology, Professor Marge Sunamoto. We're hoping she can give us some background on the first Americans.

Professor Sunamoto: Well, for a long time some scientists thought that the first people to arrive in North America walked across a land bridge over the Bering Sea about 10,000 years ago. We also thought that within 500 years their descendents had settled most of North— and even South—America.

Jon Brooks: And now?

Professor Sunamoto: Well, we're not so sure now. Lately, certain digs—places where we carefully sift through the soil—have uncovered some truly exciting clues about the first Americans.

Jon Brooks: Let's follow up on those clues with Jack Williams, our field reporter out at a dig. Jack . . .

Scene 2: A farm field in Virginia

Jack Williams: Jon, we're out here at a dig in Virginia. Our story starts when a local farmer, Harold Conover, first spotted some interesting artifacts. He contacted local authorities, and archaeologist Dr. Robert White went to the scene. And what did you find, Dr. White?

Robert White: When we saw Mr. Conover's artifacts, we were amazed! We thought they couldn't really be as old as they seemed. We started to make plans to form an excavation party that very day.

Jack Williams: I understand that so far you've found stone tools shaped for hunting, butchering, and processing game. You've also found charred bones of mud turtles and white-tailed deer. Most impressive may be the bits of charcoal left over from hunting parties cooking what they caught. Is that right, Dr. White?

Robert White: Yes.

Jack Williams: But the work is more than just finding tools, bones, and charcoal, isn't it?

Robert White: Ah, yes. The date is the most important fact. We've been able to date the campsite at about 18,000 years old. Think about it.

Jack Williams: Wow, that's truly old. Thank you for your time, Dr. White. Now, back to Jon in the studio.

Scene 3: Newsroom conference table as in Scene 1

Jon Brooks: Our thanks to Dr. Robert White for his part of the story. But there's more to come. Let's hear from our remote reporter, Miwa Huang, in South Carolina.

Scene 4: An excavation site in South Carolina

Miwa Huang: Thanks, Jon. I'm standing here at a dig in South Carolina. With me are three dig volunteers and Martin Majors, the leader of the excavation. Tell me, what prompted you to dig here?

Aimee Hazelton: It's kind of a lucky accident, really. In May of 1998, we were ready to dig at another site, but winter rains had flooded it. We came here instead.

Miwa Huang: Mr. Majors . . . ?

Martin Majors: Well, I had heard about the amazing discoveries in Virginia and elsewhere. They were really a surprise, so I thought we might find something interesting here in South Carolina.

Aimee Hazelton: I can tell you we were all excited to try to find something older than what we'd been finding.

Rashid Tikrit: We'd never looked for anything this old. We had thought that the first people had come to America around 10,000 years ago.

Ahman DeSango: Yes, it makes you wonder what we might have missed if we didn't know about the Virginia find.

Miwa Huang: So what happened?

Aimee Hazelton: Well, we were digging, and someone yelled. We all scrambled to the spot, all crowding around a tiny flake. The excitement was intense.

Martin Majors: I was in shock! I think I just stood there, staring. Right before my eyes were small flakes and small flaked tools, partially uncovered but in very old layers of dirt.

Ahman DeSango: It seemed almost too good to be true. To be safe, we dug in several nearby locations. Each time we found tools.

Rashid Tikrit: We sent our finds to be tested. We have gotten dates as far back as 15,000 to 16,000 years old. And we may find even older tools as we dig deeper.

Miwa Huang: Amazing! Well that's our story from South Carolina. Back to Jon in the studio.

Scene 5: Newsroom conference table as in Scene 1

Jon Brooks: Well done, Miwa. Professor Sunamoto, it seems that archaeologists have a new task ahead of them.

Professor Sunamoto: Yes, that's right. Not only do we need to figure out when people came to be at these sites, but also how. They may even have traveled to North America at an earlier time from another direction. We just don't know for sure.

Jon Brooks: For answers to those questions, I guess we'll have to wait until more exciting discoveries are made as people like Robert White and Martin Majors unearth more clues about the first Americans. Until next time, good day.

The End

Unit Planner

Long-Term Project Pages 14–15	Materials Needed
The First Colonies Groups research early colonies and give visual and oral presentations based on their findings. **Time Needed:** 4 weeks **Strand:** History **Lesson Link:** Chapter 3, Lesson 5; Chapter 4, Lessons 1, 2, 3, and 4	• research notebook • outline map of North America • reference materials • scissors, glue, colored pencils, crayons, and markers • Internet access • poster board
Geography Activities Pages 16–17	
Activity 1 **Where Are We Going?** Students write a logbook and journal based on their planned expedition. **Time Needed:** 30–40 minutes **Strand:** Geography **Lesson Link:** Chapter 3, Lessons 2 and 3	• outline map of the world • globe or atlas • colored pencils or markers
Activity 2 **What's in a Name?** Students use place names on a map to find evidence of Spanish culture in the southwestern United States. **Time Needed:** 30–40 minutes **Strand:** Geography **Lesson Link:** Chapter 3, Lesson 5	• colored pencils
Hands-On Activities Pages 18–19	
Activity 1 **Post-Expedition Wrap-Up** Students pretend to be explorers and prepare presentations on their expeditions. **Time Needed:** 30–40 minutes **Strand:** History **Lesson Link:** Chapter 4, Lesson 1	• outline maps of North America and South America • colored pencils • drawing paper
Activity 2 **Classroom Compact** Students make a compact, or agreement, stating rights and responsibilities for the general good of their classroom, school, and neighborhood. **Time Needed:** 30–40 minutes **Strand:** Culture **Lesson Link:** Chapter 4, Lesson 3	• pen • ink • heavy parchment paper or poster board
Performance Activity Pages 20–23	
Should We Join the Spanish? Students role-play a hypothetical meeting of Pueblo families living in New Spain in the 1600s. **Time Needed:** 30–40 minutes **Strand:** Citizenship **Lesson Link:** Chapter 3, Lesson 5	none
For Personal Finance, see pp. 108–119.	

 The First Colonies

Introduction

In this unit, students read about the first European settlements in North America. The new colonists came from different countries, and they came for different reasons, but they all had something in common. They were all trying to survive in a strange, new world. Students will research and compare early colonies.

MATERIALS

- research notebook
- reference materials
- Internet access
- outline map of North America
- poster board
- scissors, glue, colored pencils, crayons, and markers

Project Plan

Week 1: Review Early Colonies 30 minutes

Ask students to name the settlements they read about in this unit: New Spain, Roanoke, Jamestown, Plymouth, Massachusetts Bay Colony, New Netherland, and New France. Then have students brainstorm research questions about the colonies. List their research questions on the board. Tell students they will work in small groups to research one of the colonies. When their research is complete, they will give a presentation about what they learned and use the information in a class discussion to compare the colonies. Finish by organizing the class into small groups according to the colony that interests them most.

Week 2: Make a Research Plan 30–45 minutes

Have groups meet to plan their research. Encourage them to assign specific tasks to each group member. Tell them to discuss the kinds of sources and key words they will use. Suggest that students use city and county Web sites and travel sites to find out what the areas are like today. Students may find influences of the colonies in street and other place names, architectural features, and tourist sites. Remind students to keep track of their sources of information.

Week 3: Plan the Presentation 30–60 minutes

Have groups meet to share their research results and plan their presentation. Tell each group to make a poster about the colony they researched. Tell students to include the outline map with their colony marked. Then have them decorate the space around the map with words and pictures that express important ideas about the colony. Have students review their list of research questions to make sure that they include the answers on the poster or in the oral part of the presentation. Tell them to give each group member a speaking role.

Week 4: Present and Compare 30–60 minutes

Ask each group to display the poster and use it as a starting point for their presentation. After students have answered the research questions and shared other interesting facts they learned, allow time for the whole class to discuss and compare the different colonies.

Bringing Social Studies Alive
15
Use with *United States History,* Unit 2

Name _____ Date _____

 # Where Are We Going?

Early explorers often set out on journeys not fully knowing where the journey would end or what they might find along the way. However, later explorers were able to use the information left behind by the first explorers. The later explorers had a better idea of where to go, how to get there, and what they might find during their journeys. You can be an explorer and use information you have learned to explore a region.

MATERIALS

- outline map of the world
- globe or atlas
- colored pencils or markers

1. In groups of four, use a globe or atlas to choose a destination.

2. Together, use the world maps in your atlas or a globe to plan the best route to the destination from where you live. Create your plans using only land and water routes.

3. Mark your route on the outline map of the world.

4. Read the captain's logbook headings below. Discuss possible entries with your fellow explorers. Then complete the logbook entries together.

Travel Plans

We're headed for _____.

We'll leave from our hometown of _____.

We'll use _____ as methods of transportation.

We expect to cover _____ miles.

We expect to see _____.

Write a journal entry describing one day of the journey. Share your entry with the other groups.

16   Use with *United States History*, Unit 2

Name _____ Date _____

 # What's in a Name?

Place names such as Death Valley or Sandy Creek reveal information about the geography of a location. In the same way, place names such as Earl's Gulch and Johnstown can reveal information about the people of a region. The southwestern United States has hundreds of place names that reflect the region's early Spanish influences. Look at the map below to find evidence of Spanish culture.

<table>
<tr><td>MATERIALS</td></tr>
<tr><td>• colored pencils</td></tr>
</table>

Use the map to answer the following questions. Write your answers on the map or on the back of this worksheet.

1. Shade the region that Spain claimed as part of New Spain.

2. Find Del Rio, Texas, on the map. The name means "of the river" in Spanish. On what river is Del Rio located?

3. The original name of El Paso, Texas, was El Paso del Norte, meaning "The Pass of the North" in Spanish. El Paso is located where Texas, New Mexico, and the Rio Grande meet. Mark the location of El Paso, Texas, on the map.

4. The Spanish gave the Rio Grande the name Rio de Las Palmas, which means "river of the palms." The Mexican name for the Rio Grande is Rio Bravo, which means "great river" or "wild river." What do these names tell you about the river and the climate of its valley?

17

Name _____   Date _____

 # Post-Expedition Wrap-Up

Introduction

When early explorers returned home, they were summoned to make a report of their journey to their kings and queens. Now you will put yourself in the role of an explorer and prepare a presentation of the details of your latest expedition.

Getting Started

1. Reread the expeditions described in this unit. Choose an expedition that you thought was interesting or exciting.

2. Find out all you can about the expedition that you chose.

3. Make a short list of the details about the expedition. For example, what was the weather like during the journey? What landforms did the expedition explore? What plants and animals were observed? How can the information gathered be valuable to the king and queen?

4. Present your findings to a classmate. Use a map to show where you explored.

Checklist

☐ 1. My presentation shows the variety of plants and animals seen on the expedition.

☐ 2. My presentation shows the variety of landforms.

☐ 3. My presentation lists several suggestions for moneymaking enterprises involving the explored lands.

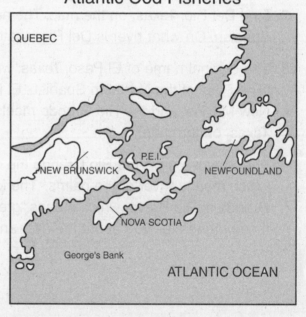

Atlantic Cod Fisheries

QUEBEC

NEW BRUNSWICK

P.E.I.

NOVA SCOTIA

NEWFOUNDLAND

George's Bank

ATLANTIC OCEAN

Name _____ Date _____

Classroom Compact

Introduction

When the Pilgrims landed in Massachusetts, they made a compact, or agreement, to make and follow laws for the "general good" of the settlement. You can make your own compact stating the rights and responsibilities for the general good of your classroom, school, and neighborhood.

MATERIALS

- pen
- ink
- heavy parchment paper or poster board

Getting Started

1. Form three committees, one each for *classroom*, *school*, and *neighborhood*. Each committee should discuss the rights and responsibilities of the people who share their place.

2. Make a list of the rights and responsibilities that apply to your place.

3. Put your list to the test. Think of a real-life problem. Solve the problem by applying your rights and responsibilities.

4. Make a compact for your place on parchment paper or poster board.

5. Meet as a class. Share your compact and your problem and solution with the other committees.

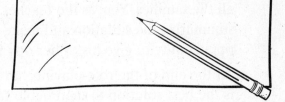

1. Classroom rights, classroom responsibilities

2. School rights, school responsibilities

3. Neighborhood rights, neighborhood responsibilities

Checklist

☐ 1. My committee listed several group rights.

☐ 2. My committee listed several group responsibilities.

☐ 3. My committee made a compact with guidelines for sharing a place with others.

 # Should We Join the Spanish?

Simulation Overview

In this simulation, students will role-play a hypothetical meeting of Pueblo families living in New Spain in the 1600s.

Procedures

- Distribute the simulation overview and discuss with students. Make certain that students understand the basic situation, the dilemma in which the Pueblo families find themselves, and the purpose of the meeting.

- Form five family groups. Allow each group time to discuss its position. Each family group should appoint a leader. That leader should encourage family members to develop and list several relevant arguments to support the family's position.

- Direct each family leader to choose two or three other family members to present the family's position to the entire class. One person can explain the action the family wishes to take, while the others give reasons for the decision, adding appropriate details. Be certain students have enough time to prepare what they will say.

- After each family has prepared its presentation, begin a meeting of all the families. You, as the teacher, can lead the meeting. Briefly summarize the situation and make sure every family member has an opportunity to give his or her opinion.

- At the end of the role-playing, have students vote on what they think is the best solution to the Pueblo families' dilemma.

Overview

For years, American Indians in New Spain struggled with the choices they faced as the Spanish took over their land.

In the past few years, you have heard rumors of European conquerors bringing settlers, soldiers, and priests to your region. You've heard that when these people come, American Indians have been forced to farm or work in mines. You've also heard that American Indians were often cheated out of their hard-earned pay.

One priest has convinced the king to pass laws to protect American Indian rights. However, most settlers ignore the laws.

Some of your neighbors have already moved to the missions. You've heard rumors of a plan to revolt near your home in New Mexico.

Your family, and many other families, are concerned about the future. You and your family are meeting to discuss your options. You will then meet with other neighboring families to discuss the best action to take.

Family 1: Do Nothing

Your family does not believe the rumors that have reached the region. You cannot believe that anyone could force you off your land or make you give up your traditions. You think that these stories are exaggerations and that you can continue to live in your region and farm your lands as your family has for centuries. Besides, you have also heard that there are now laws against stealing from American Indians. You intend to stay and continue practicing your traditions and religion.

Good things about this idea:

_____

_____

Possible problems with this point of view:

_____

_____

Family 2: Move to a Mission

Your family and neighbors believe it is in your best interest to go along with the Spanish. You feel that it is not too great a sacrifice to move to the missions and to learn the Spanish language and customs if it will keep your family safe. You've heard that some of the priests are kind and offer protection from some of the other settlers.

Good things about this idea:

_____

_____

Possible problems with this point of view:

_____

✂ –

Group 3: Revolt

You are concerned about your family members being made to work in the mines. Mining is difficult and dangerous work. In addition, you do not want to give up your land and your way of life to learn the Spanish language and customs. You want the Spanish to leave. You are willing to join with others in a revolt. If enough American Indians join forces, you feel that you will be able to drive away the settlers.

Good things about this idea:

_____

_____

Possible problems with this point of view:

_____

_____

Group 4: Move to Another Region

You believe the rumors are true, and you do not wish to give up your religion and traditions. However, you are concerned that you and your friends may not be able to defeat the Spanish. After all, they have more powerful weapons. If you move farther north, or perhaps farther east, you may be able to escape the Spanish. You may be able to build new pueblos and live, work, and farm as you have for centuries.

Good things about this idea:

_____

_____

Possible problems with this point of view:

_____

_____

Group 5: Undecided

Your family understands the choices available to you and your extended family. You can continue to live as you have for centuries and hope that the Spanish will not come. You may decide to join the Spanish and give up your old beliefs. You would like to fight the settlers and drive them out, but you are not certain you could win. If you move east or north, you may find more Europeans. Besides, you don't know if the land in these places is good for farming. You decide to try to think of another way to solve this problem.

Possible solution:

_____

_____

Unit Planner

Long-Term Project Pages 26–27	Materials Needed
Children of Colonial Times Groups research what everyday life was like for colonial children and create a presentation based on their findings. **Time Needed:** 4 weeks **Strand:** Culture **Lesson Link:** Chapter 5, Lesson 3; Chapter 6, Lessons 2 and 4	• Internet and library access, encyclopedias • drawing paper • posterboard • colored pencils, crayons, and markers
Geography Activities Pages 28–29	
Activity 1 **Produce a Product Map** Students make a product and resource map to show what was available in the colonies. **Time Needed:** 30–40 minutes **Strand:** Geography **Lesson Link:** Chapter 5, Lesson 3; Chapter 6, Lessons 2 and 4	• outline map of the 13 colonies • colored pencils or markers
Activity 2 **Settlement Patterns** Students answer questions using a map of the colonies showing the homelands of immigrant groups. **Time Needed:** 30–40 minutes **Strand:** Geography **Lesson Link:** Chapter 5, Lesson 1; Chapter 6, Lessons 1, 2, and 3	none
Hands-On Activities Pages 30–31	
Activity 1 **Trading Cod for Cloth** Students play a card game in which they trade goods between the Colonies, England, and the West Indies triangle. **Time Needed:** 30–40 minutes **Strand:** Economics **Lesson Link:** Chapter 5, Lesson 3	• outline map of the world • colored markers or pencils • index cards
Activity 2 **Wish You Were Here!** Students create a handbill encouraging people to immigrate to their settlements. **Time Needed:** 30–40 minutes **Strand:** Culture **Lesson Link:** Chapter 5, Lessons 1 and 2; Chapter 6, Lessons 1 and 3	• drawing paper • colored markers • information about life in the colonies
Performance Activity Pages 32–35	
Where Should We Go? Students role-play a secret meeting of Quakers during which they decide where to go to escape persecution. **Time Needed:** 30–40 minutes **Strand:** Citizenship **Lesson Link:** Chapter 5, Lesson 2	none
For Personal Finance, see pp. 108–119.	

Children of Colonial Times

Introduction

Students can associate their daily lives with the lives of colonial children if they know about everyday colonial life. Students will research different aspects of the lives of colonial children and give presentations.

MATERIALS

- Internet and library access, encyclopedia
- drawing paper
- posterboard
- colored pencils, crayons, and markers

Project Plan

Week 1: Discuss Colonial Times 20–30 minutes

Open a class discussion about what students generally have for breakfast, at what hour they wake, and when they go to bed. Then ask students to speculate how similar or different these habits might be if they lived in colonial America. Ask students the following:

- How might they find out about everyday colonial life?
- What kinds of references could they use to find out what colonial children ate for breakfast?
- Where would they look to find out how colonial children dressed?
- What toys and games were available?

Record students' responses on the chalkboard. Have them suggest key words they might use to search an encyclopedia, library card catalog, or the Internet. Encourage students to record key words on paper.

Week 2: Research 30–60 minutes

Direct students to form groups of three or four. Assign to each group one of the thirteen colonies or regions of the colonies. Tell students that they should answer these questions:

- What did colonial children eat for breakfast? Lunch? Dinner?
- What did colonial children study? Did they study at home or in school?
- What clothes did colonial children wear?
- What games or toys did colonial children enjoy?
- What chores did colonial children do?

Allow student groups time to discuss research strategies, including what sources and key words they will use. Indicate to students that they may want to assign specific tasks to individual group members. Have students do the research and take notes.

Week 3: Plan Presentation and Make Visuals 30–60 minutes

Have each group determine the best way to present its findings. For example, students may draw a breakfast scene, construct a facsimile of a hornbook, or present paper dolls of children's clothes. If appropriate, groups may demonstrate colonial games such as jackstraws or blindman's buff. Remind students that they should indicate the sources they used to support their findings.

Week 4: Present Findings 30–45 minutes

Have each group present its findings to the whole class. After the presentations, have students discuss how their lives are similar to and different from the lives of colonial children.

Bringing Social Studies Alive
27
Use with *United States History,* Unit 3

Name _____ Date _____

Produce a Product Map

Many early colonists struggled to make a living. The crops they could grow and the resources they could use to manufacture items were different throughout the colonies. Make a product and resource map showing the farm and manufactured products available in different regions of the colonies.

MATERIALS

- outline map of the 13 colonies
- colored pencils or markers

1. Divide into three groups: New England Colonies, Middle Colonies, and Southern Colonies. Within each group, work with a partner.

2. Depending on your region, reread the Life in New England, Life in the Middle Colonies, or Life in the South lesson in your textbook.

3. Working with your partner, make a list of at least three crops and/or animals that colonists in your region raised to feed their own families. Make a second list of at least three cash crops, resources, and/or industries that the colonists used to make a living.

4. Develop a symbol to represent each item on your list. Draw the symbols on your region on the outline map. Create a legend for the map that shows what each symbol means.

5. Write three questions that can be answered using your map. Trade maps with pairs that made maps on the other two regions. Answer each other's questions.

Name _____ Date _____

 # Settlement Patterns

The early colonists tended to live in areas where people from their homelands had already settled. The settlement patterns of the colonists can be shown on an immigrant map.

Use the map and information from your textbook to answer the questions. Write your answers on the map or on the back of this paper.

1. Which symbol on the map represents English immigrants? Label the symbol.

2. One of the symbols is "Other." This symbol includes Dutch immigrants. Use what you learned about New Jersey and New York to identify the "Other" symbol. Label the symbol.

3. Use the information in your textbook and the distance scale on the map to draw in the *fall line* for the colonies.

4. The Scotch-Irish tended to settle near the fall line and close to the frontier. Which of the symbols represents the Scotch-Irish immigrants? Label the symbol.

5. The remaining symbol is "Welsh." In what colonies were Welsh immigrants concentrated?

6. From which immigrant group were most of the people in South Carolina?

7. Some people chose to settle on the frontier. What would be some advantages and disadvantages of settling there?

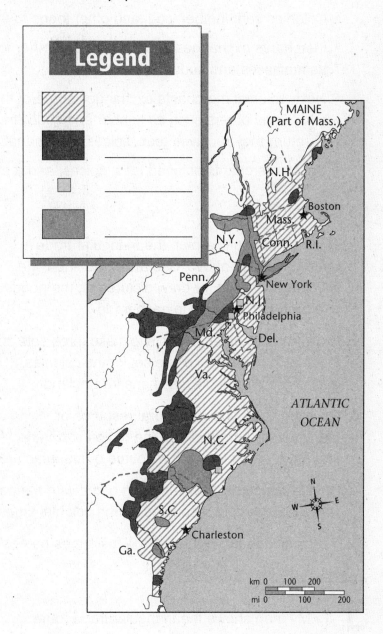

Name _____ Date _____

 # Trading Cod for Cloth

Introduction

By the 1700s, American colonists had developed trading
routes with other places to obtain the goods and resources
the colonies did not have.

- Colonies sent lumber, cod, and other foods to the West Indies.

- Merchants exchanged lumber, cod, and other foods for goods such
  as molasses and sugar.

- Next, colonial merchants exchanged some of the West Indian
  goods and others such as lumber and cod with British merchants.
  In return they received teas, spices, and manufactured goods.

- British merchants shipped teas, spices, and manufactured goods.

Getting Started

1. Trace on the outline map the triangular trade
   route described above. Use arrows to show the
   flow of goods. List, or draw pictures of, the goods
   and products involved in each trade.

2. Work with two other students to make three sets of
   ten trading cards. Make one set for the colonies,
   one for the West Indies, and one for England.

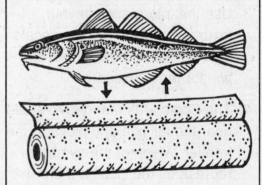

3. On each card, show a natural resource or
   manufactured product that the region can trade.
   Make two cards for each resource or manufactured product.

4. Shuffle the cards. Play a trading game with them as if you were
   trading goods and resources during colonial times.

5. Play until one player has all the resources he or she needs.

Checklist

☐ 1. My map shows the triangular trade route.

☐ 2. The products or resources traded are shown on my map.

☐ 3. The game cards show resources or products that the colonists
     traded.

Bringing Social Studies Alive

Use with *United States History*, Unit 3

Name _____ Date _____

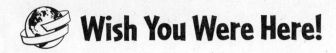 **Wish You Were Here!**

Introduction

Settlers from England, Germany, Scotland, Ireland, the Netherlands, Sweden, and Wales moved into particular regions of the 13 colonies. They often received letters from friends and family wondering if they, too, should come to the colonies. You, acting as a settler, can help them decide. Prepare a handbill—a sheet of paper with information printed on it that is generally handed out to people—telling about your settlement.

MATERIALS

- drawing paper
- colored markers
- information about life in the colonies

Getting Started

- Together with three other students, choose one of the following communities:

    — a Dutch community along the Hudson River

    — a Puritan community in Massachusetts

    — a Quaker community in Pennsylvania

    — an English community in Virginia

- Design and write a handbill giving reasons that you, as settlers in that community, feel others should join you. Include at least three of the following:

    — a news event from one of the colonies

    — a statement indicating how and why additional settlers will benefit from the move

    — a cartoon or illustration of your settlement

    — quotations from a variety of people, such as farmers, merchants, or the governor

Checklist

☐ 1. My handbill is easy to read and full of facts.

☐ 2. My handbill contains three required items.

☐ 3. My handbill could be used to persuade people to come to my colony.

 # Where Should We Go?

Simulation Overview

In this simulation, students role-play a hypothetical meeting of a group of the Society of Friends, known as Quakers, in a small Connecticut town in the early 1660s.

Procedures

- Distribute the simulation overview and discuss it with students. Make certain students understand the basic situation, the difficulties in which the Quakers find themselves, and the purpose of the meeting.

- Form five groups. Allow each group time to discuss its position. Each group should appoint a leader who will help the group develop several relevant arguments to support the group's position. The leader should list the arguments.

- Direct each group leader to choose two or three other group members to present their group's position to the entire class. One person can explain the action the family wishes to take, while the others give reasons for it, adding appropriate details. Be certain students have enough time to prepare what they will say.

- After each group has prepared its presentation, begin the meeting. You, as the teacher, can lead the meeting. Briefly summarize the situation and make sure every family member has an opportunity to give his or her opinion.

- At the end of the role-playing, have students vote on what they think is the best solution to the Quakers' problem.

Overview

You are a member of a group of Quakers who have been living and meeting in your town of Millbrook, Connecticut. You came to the colonies because the religious persecution in England prevented you from holding your meetings. Now, in the colonies, you find you are facing some of the same problems. The Puritans, the major religious group in New England, seem to have little or no tolerance for Quakers. Quakers are often imprisoned or fined. They are generally treated cruelly.

People who are Quakers are pacifists. That is, they live peacefully and believe that violence toward others is wrong. Even so, during the last few months, several people, presumed to be Quakers, have experienced violence in Millbrook. Some have had stones thrown at them; others have found angry letters nailed to their doors. The persecution is becoming widespread and is turning into a serious problem. It is becoming dangerous for Quakers to live in Millbrook. Many members of your group are worried about their safety and the safety of their families.

The purpose of your meeting today is to decide how the Quakers of Millbrook should deal with this problem. In Quaker meetings, anyone who wishes is allowed to speak. As a result, several different suggestions have been made about what your group should do.

- ✂ - - -

Group 1: Protest

Your group wants to stay in Millbrook and openly practice your religion. You think that any kind of religious persecution is unfair. You feel that you should not be forced to leave your hometown for no good reason.

Good things about this idea: _____

_____

Possible problems with this point of view: _____

_____

Group 2: Talk It Over

Your group wants to stay in Millbrook and continue to meet. You wish to meet with people in Millbrook who have been persecuting you. You hope that they will see that you are no threat to the community and want to live in peace.

Good things about this idea: _____

_____

Possible problems with this point of view: _____

_____

Group 3: Get Out of Town

People in your group want to move to Rhode Island, which allows religious freedom for all of its citizens. You are tired of being persecuted by the Connecticut government and your neighbors. You want to start new lives in a place where you will not have to be secretive about your religious beliefs.

Good things about this idea: _____

_____

Possible problems with this point of view: _____

_____

Group 4: Join the Millbrook Church

Your group has decided to stop meeting as Quakers and to become active members of the Millbrook church. You think that there are more similarities than differences between yourselves and the other citizens of Millbrook. You plan to keep your Quaker beliefs in your hearts but go along with the town's religious beliefs in your daily life.

Good things about this idea: _____

_____

Possible problems with this point of view: _____

_____

Group 5: Undecided

Your group sees many possible choices for Millbrook's Quakers. One possibility would be to move to Rhode Island, where all religions are welcome. Another would be to stay in Millbrook and to protest the unfair treatment of Quakers in Connecticut. What other possibilities can you think of? Make a list of possible solutions to share with the other groups. Remember that it is important to find a solution that everyone can accept.

Possible solutions: _____

_____

Unit Planner

Long-Term Project Pages 38–39	
Create Cartoons About Taxes Students research colonial taxation and create cartoons displaying their findings. **Time Needed:** 4 weeks **Strand:** Economics **Lesson Link:** Chapter 7, Lessons 2 and 3	• political cartoons from newspapers • paper • colored pens and pencils • markers
Geography Activities Pages 40–41	
Activity 1 **Saratoga Battle Plan** Students make a map of the planned and actual routes of the British forces at the Battle of Saratoga. **Time Needed:** 30–40 minutes **Strand:** Geography **Lesson Link:** Chapter 8, Lesson 3	• colored pencils
Activity 2 **Blockade!** Students make a map of communication and transportation locations in their community in order to understand what a blockade would mean to their area. **Time Needed:** 30–40 minutes **Strand:** Geography **Lesson Link:** Chapter 7, Lesson 4	• a map of your community, state, or region • drawing paper • colored pencils or markers
Hands-On Activities Pages 42–43	
Activity 1 **Make a Diorama** Students research and build a diorama of a Revolutionary War battle. **Time Needed:** 30–40 minutes **Strand:** History **Lesson Link:** Chapter 7, Lessons, 1, 2, 3, and 4 Chapter 8, Lessons 3 and 4	• empty shoebox or other box • paints • paper • clay • soldiers (plastic, clay, or paper) • scissors • paste or glue
Activity 2 **Make a Primary Source Artifact** Students create a handwritten "original" document of an amendment to the Constitution. **Time Needed:** 30–40 minutes **Strand:** History **Lesson Link:** Chapter 9, Lesson 2	• pen and ink or thin-tipped markers • heavy paper
Performance Activity Pages 44–47	
A Meeting in Philadelphia Students put on a play about the Constitutional Convention in Philadelphia. **Time Needed:** 30–40 minutes **Strand:** Citizenship **Lesson Link:** Chapter 9, Lesson 2	none
For Personal Finance, see pp. 108–119.	

Bringing Social Studies Alive

37

Use with *United States History*, Unit 4

Create Cartoons About Taxes

Introduction

Even before the French and Indian War, the British government extracted a variety of "taxes" from the colonies. Most of these aimed to control trade rather than to raise revenue. For example, in 1660 the British identified specific items— including sugar, indigo, and tobacco—that could be shipped only to other English possessions. In addition, the British demanded duties be paid on some of these goods. During the next 115 years, the British Crown levied a variety of duties or taxes on colonial goods.

Project Plan

Week 1: Discuss Taxes and Duties 30–45 minutes

Open a class discussion about how the British used duties to control trade and raise revenue. Tell students that they can create a series of tax cartoons to show how the British attempted to control the finances of the colonies and generate revenue for the crown. Show students some political cartoons from newspapers and discuss the cartoons.

Week 2: Research Taxes 30–45 minutes

Have students form five research-and-report groups. Each group should investigate one of the following British laws: the Staple Act, the Molasses Act, the Stamp Act, the Townshend Act, and the Tea Act. Direct groups to research taxes levied by the British and paid (or avoided) by the colonists for each of these laws. Tell students that their reports should include colonists' reaction to the financial obligations. Tell them to find, if possible, the official wording of the law or a quotation from a member of Parliament or a colonist regarding the tax.

Encourage students to use a variety of sources. Remind students to record where they found their information. Students may also wish to print or draw visuals they find during their research.

Week 3: Create a Cartoon and Description 30–45 minutes

Direct students to review their research and work together to produce a tax-related cartoon. Groups should consider ideas such as showing a tax being levied and the colonists' reaction to the tax collector. Each cartoon should be accompanied by a description of the tax, what it was meant to do, and how it was received in the colonies. Descriptions should also include any appropriate first-person quotations.

Groups may also wish to explore some of the more unusual taxes between 1600 and 1800—for example, window, hair powder, and salt taxes. They could then present their extra research on posters.

Week 4: Share Cartoons 30–60 minutes

Place cartoons and posters around the classroom for viewing. Allow time for students to view one another's cartoons up close and in detail. Then invite a representative of each group to describe the taxes they researched. Remind the representatives to tell what commodities were involved as well as the purpose of the tax. Have students who produced posters present the background story for the posters.

Saratoga Battle Plan

The Patriots defeated the British forces, led by General Burgoyne, at Saratoga in 1777. You can use the map below, the description of the British plan, and the actual troop movements to show how the Patriots won.

MATERIALS

• colored pencils

Planned Routes

The British plan to attack Saratoga consisted of three major parts. Colonel St. Leger was to travel east from Oswego through the Mohawk River Valley. Sir William Howe was to travel north up the Hudson River from New York City. General Burgoyne planned to travel south from Canada, down Lake Champlain and the Hudson River.

Actual Routes

St. Leger started eastward and attacked Fort Stanwix. American General Benedict Arnold tricked St. Leger's troops and forced them back to Oswego. Rather than travel north, Howe decided to attack Philadelphia. Burgoyne followed the original plan. He and his troops engaged the Patriot forces at Saratoga. However, no British reinforcements came from either the south or the west. Burgoyne eventually surrendered.

1. On another sheet of paper, make a legend to show the routes of the three British commanders. Use a different color for each commander. Use solid lines to show planned routes. Use dotted lines to show actual routes.

2. Draw the planned and actual routes on the map.

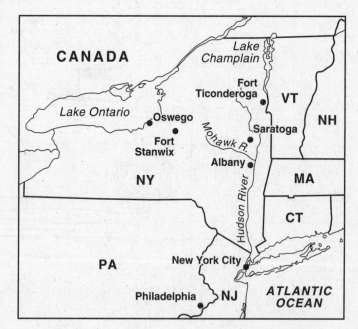

Blockade!

In 1774, the British moved to punish Boston for the Boston Tea Party. They blockaded Boston Harbor. No food or goods from across the Atlantic or from other American colonies could enter Boston Harbor. The blockade also stopped goods from leaving Boston. Massachusetts colonists had to adapt to the blockade. Many began to weave their own cloth. Fishing boats remained in port and export of cattle and other livestock stopped. Many colonists were put out of work because manufacturers stopped producing goods.

MATERIALS

- a map of your community, state, or region
- drawing paper
- colored pencils or markers

Suppose a blockade cut off your community from the rest of the world. No news, food, or other goods could reach you. How would you and your community adapt to the blockade?

1. Make a list of the different ways that goods and information reach your community, such as on roads and highways or from the radio station. Which transportation and communication systems would have to be blocked to cut off, or isolate, your community?

2. Make a sketch based on the map of your state or region. On your sketch, mark the location of important transportation and communication centers. Identify those that you think would be the most difficult to blockade.

3. Make a list of incoming goods and services that would be affected by the blockade. What goods might still be available? Make another list showing the outgoing goods and services that would be affected. Which would not be affected?

4. Which goods or services would you miss the most? Can you think of substitutes for them? What would happen as a result of not being able to ship products from your region?

Name _____ Date _____

HANDS ON ACTIVITY

Make a Diorama

Introduction

In this unit, you read about many important battles fought during the American Revolutionary War. You can bring a part of the Revolutionary War to life as you design a diorama showing a scene of one of these important battles.

Getting Started

1. Review the battles described in this unit. Choose a battle you think was particularly important or unusual.

2. Find out all you can about the battle you chose. Reread the information in your textbook. Look for other information about the battle in other books or on the Internet. If you use the Internet, remember to use only Web sites approved by your teacher or librarian.

3. Make a short list of the details about the battle. For example, what was the weather like during the battle? How did the geography of the site affect battle strategy? Which armies took part? What did their uniforms look like? Which army had the greater number of soldiers? How did the weapons of opposing armies compare? Who won the battle?

Checklist

☐ 1. My diorama shows a real battle from the American Revolution.

☐ 2. My diorama shows at least three interesting details about the battle.

☐ 3. My diorama uses at least three different art materials, such as paper, plastic soldiers, and clay.

Bringing Social Studies Alive

42

Use with *United States History*, Unit 4

Name _____ Date _____

Make a Primary Source Artifact

Introduction

Today when we read the Constitution or the Bill of Rights, we usually read text that has been reproduced by a mechanical or electronic printer. The original documents were written by a person using pen and ink. See for yourself how history can come to life through a handwritten "original."

Getting Started

1. Read the Bill of Rights on pages 334–335 of your textbook. Choose one of the amendments to record in your own handwriting.

2. Decide how you can make your written document look official. Will it have a title? Will it have a seal or ribbon? Will there be signatures at the bottom?

3. Have a classmate read the amendment to you. Write the words as if you are recording the amendment for future generations.

4. Display the amendment, along with those of your classmates, on a classroom wall. Also display a printed version of the document. Discuss what features of the handwritten documents make them look official.

Checklist

- [ ] 1. My written document is part of the Bill of Rights.

- [ ] 2. My written amendment is accurate.

- [ ] 3. My written amendment has at least two features that make it look official.

Bringing Social Studies Alive

43

Use with *United States History*, Unit 4

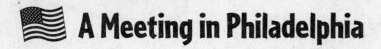

A Meeting in Philadelphia

How do people write a plan for a form of government that is new to the world? In the summer of 1787, delegates from several states held a Constitutional Convention in Philadelphia. The meetings produced the Constitution of the United States.

In addition to the final document, we have descriptions of the delegates' day-by-day discussions. Some delegates, such as James Madison, took notes during the meetings. From their notes we know that George Washington was chosen to chair the meeting. We can also guess that their meetings might have sounded like the following.

Cast of Characters

George Washington:	delegate from Virginia and meeting chair
Edmund Randolph:	delegate from Virginia
Alexander Hamilton:	delegate from New York
James Madison:	delegate from Virginia
William Livingston:	delegate from New Jersey
Rufus King:	delegate from Massachusetts
Roger Sherman:	delegate from Connecticut
Abraham Baldwin:	delegate from Georgia
Pierce Butler:	delegate from South Carolina

Scene 1: Another day of debate

George Washington *(wearily):* Gentlemen, welcome back. As you know, we've been debating the Virginia Plan for many days. In effect, we must decide if our task is to revise our existing confederation or create a new national government. We must find a way to establish a strong central government.

[William Livingston raises his hand.]

George Washington: Mr. Livingston, what does New Jersey have to say on the matter?

William Livingston: I wish to emphasize that we must have a strong central government. I believe that a weak government and rampant local interests will give us a government no better than the government offered by the Crown.

George Washington: Precisely so. But in the quest for a strong central, or federal, government, we must be certain not to infringe on the rights of the individual states. Key to that task is how states will be represented in this new national government.

[Edmund Randolph raises his hand.]

George Washington: Mr. Randolph, what does Virginia have to say on the matter?

Edmund Randolph: Sir, Mr. Madison and I propose a federal government with three different parts, or branches. One branch, a Congress, would make the laws, another branch would interpret the laws, and a third branch would carry out the laws.

Alexander Hamilton: That's a fine suggestion. Many of our own state governments already use a similar structure. But how will the states be represented in this Congress?

Abraham Baldwin: States could have representation according to the number of property owners on record.

James Madison: As you say, the number of representatives could reflect the population of each state. That way, states with greater populations will have a greater number of representatives in Congress. That seems only fair.

William Livingston: Oh no! I thoroughly disagree! In fact, the very idea offends me! I come from New Jersey, a smaller state. Are we to have less say in the government just because we are smaller? Are you saying that my state isn't important?

Roger Sherman: Indeed, as a representative of Connecticut I too see the scheme as unfair to smaller states. If this body continues to pursue that idea, I'm afraid that Connecticut will have to withdraw from these proceedings.

George Washington: Mr. Livingston, Mr. Sherman, please! Calm down. Of course your states are important. No one is suggesting otherwise. Your idea, Mr. Livingston?

William Livingston: It seems obvious to me that every state should send one and only one delegate to Congress. That way, every state has an equal amount of power in the federal government. One state, one vote. It's the only way.

Rufus King: That's ridiculous! Absolutely not! I represent a state with a greater population than some others. I cannot accept a scheme that does not allow the people of Massachusetts to be properly represented in the new government. Sir, are you suggesting that we ignore population entirely? Preposterous!

[All delegates begin to argue and speak loudly at the same time.]

George Washington: Gentlemen, gentlemen, please! We will not solve the problem by arguing. I suggest we take some time to think the problem over. We can meet again tomorrow to continue the discussion. And, if luck is with us, we will find a fair solution to the representation problem.

Scene 2: Reaching a compromise

George Washington: Gentlemen, shall we pick up our discussion of the structure of the new Congress? Any new ideas?

[Roger Sherman raises his hand.]

George Washington: Mr. Sherman, what can Connecticut add to this discussion?

Roger Sherman: Well, as you remember we have already agreed to have a government with three branches: one to make laws, one to interpret laws, and one to carry out laws. Well, in the same way, I propose that we have two branches of Congress.

Edmund Randolph: What? What good will that do? Divisions within divisions? I thought we were trying to form a strong, united government.

Roger Sherman: Ah, respectfully, Sir, that is my point. Suppose we have two branches of Congress. One branch, called the Senate, would represent each state equally. Say, one or two representatives from each state. This would mean that each state would be equally represented.

Abraham Baldwin: Go on.

Roger Sherman: Then the second branch, or House of Representatives, would consist of a number of delegates from each state. That is, states would be represented according to their population. This way all our constituents would be suitably represented.

[A general murmur arises from delegates as they turn the idea over in their minds.]

Pierce Butler: I see . . . That way, each state has a strong voice, but population is also represented. That bodes well. This will help us fashion the strong central government we need to gain international respect and economic growth.

Rufus King: Excellent! It is a good and worthy plan. Thank you, Mr. Sherman. I did not believe this problem could be solved, yet you seem to have done it.

George Washington: Shall we put it to a vote? Right then. Will delegates in favor of Mr. Sherman's suggestion please say "Aye."

All delegates: Aye.

George Washington: Then we will include two houses of Congress in our Constitution—one based on a state's existence and one based on a state's population.

James Madison: Sirs, let us emphasize as we bring this document back to our constituents that it is not the offspring of a single brain but the work of many heads and many hands.

George Washington: Quite so. Quite so. We have accomplished much through compromise. Let us turn to the next task at hand.

The End

Unit Planner

Long-Term Project Pages 50–51	**Materials Needed**
The Best President Students define and present information on what makes a good president. **Time Needed:** 4 weeks **Strand:** Citizenship **Lesson Link:** Chapter 10, Lessons 2, 3, and 4 Chapter 11, Lesson 3	• Internet access and other research materials • research notebook • presentation materials • research data • art materials
Geography Activities Pages 52–53	
Activity 1 **Traveling West** Students make a three-dimensional landform map of the route the pioneers used when traveling west. **Time Needed:** 30–40 minutes **Strand:** Geography **Lesson Link:** Chapter 11, Lesson 4	• tracing paper • modeling clay • string • tape • cardboard
Activity 2 **Plan a Trip to California** Students use a map to plan a road trip from Chicago to California. **Time Needed:** 30–40 minutes **Strand:** Geography **Lesson Link:** Chapter 11, Lesson 4	• U.S. highway map
Hands-On Activity Pages 54–55	
Build a Paddlewheel Boat Students make models of a paddlewheel boat. **Time Needed:** 30–40 minutes **Strand:** History **Lesson Link:** Chapter 11, Lesson 1	• cardboard • scissors • rubber band • stapler • waterproof paint (optional)
Performance Activity Pages 56–59	
Rip Van Winkle Students put on a play about Rip Van Winkle. **Time Needed:** 30–40 minutes **Strand:** Culture **Lesson Link:** Chapter 10, Lesson 3	• props optional: • stick to represent hunting rifle • ball • doll • 2 large bundles • fake gray beard
For Personal Finance, see pp. 108–119.	

 The Best President

Introduction

MATERIALS

- Internet access and other research materials
- research notebook
- presentation materials
- research data, art materials

In Unit 5, students learn about events that transpired during the terms of six early Presidents. Challenge students to define what makes a good President. Then have them make presentations about each President and vote on which of the six Presidents was the best.

Project Plan

Week 1: What Makes a Good President? 30 minutes

Discuss with students the characteristics and actions that make a President successful. Encourage students to discuss topics such as the President's position on issues, the country's progress, the people's welfare and satisfaction, the President's leadership qualities, the people's feelings about the President at the time, and the lasting effects of the President's term. Have students take notes during the discussion and then write a list of criteria for judging what makes a good President.

List the Presidents discussed in Unit 5: Thomas Jefferson, James Madison, James Monroe, Andrew Jackson, Martin Van Buren, and James Polk. Invite students to discuss what they know about each President.

Organize the class into groups and assign one President to each group.

Week 2: Research a President 30–45 minutes

Have students research the President who was assigned to their group. Suggest that they begin by reading what the textbook says to find out about major events that the President had to deal with during his term of office.

Encourage students to use the Internet, encyclopedias, and other classroom and library resources to find out more about their President. Suggest that the research include the President's positions on American Indians, slavery, expansionism, and war with other countries. Remind students to keep in mind their criteria for judging a good President.

Allow a few minutes at the end of the period for students to meet and discuss their findings.

Week 3: Plan a Presentation 30–45 minutes

Have students in each gropu meet to review what they learned from their research. Tell students to organize their information according to the criteria they established for judging a President. Point out that within each gropu, students may form different conclusions about their President.

Then have the groups of students prepare a presentation about their President. Remind them to present major events that occurred during the President's term, the President's position on issues, the satisfaction or dissatisfaction of the people, whether or not the President was reelected to a second term, and lasting effects of the President's actions.

Tell students to prepare visual aids, such as drawings or public domain photographs of the President, maps that show the size of the country and its territories during the President's term, graphs, or charts. Students may make visuals by hand that are large enough to be seen throughout the room, or they may prefer to make transparencies on a computer to be projected onto a screen or chalkboard.

Week 4: Discuss and Vote 30–45 minutes

Have each group present the results of their research to the class during a panel discussion.

After all the groups have made their presentations, invite the class to vote on which of the six Presidents was the best President. Remind students that they will not be voting for the best group or best presentation. Instead they should use their criteria for judging a President to vote on the best President.

After the vote has been taken, have students explain their opinions.

Traveling West

Make a Landform Map

In the 1800s, pioneers were on the move. They were moving west for many reasons. These travelers followed established trails. Even so, the routes west were long and difficult. Making a three-dimensional model of the landforms that stood in their way can help you understand just how difficult the journey was.

MATERIALS

- tracing paper
- modeling clay
- string
- tape
- sheet of cardboard

Make a Map

Follow these steps to make a landform map that shows some trails the pioneers used.

1. Use tracing or other paper to trace the United States physical map in the textbook's Atlas. Tape your map to the sheet of cardboard.

2. Make clay mountains on the map. Use clay to show other landforms the pioneers had to cross. Use the Atlas map as a guide.

3. Look at the trail map on page 402. Lay pieces of string across your map to show the Oregon Trail, the Santa Fe Trail, the California Trail, and the Mormon Trail. Press each piece of string into the clay.

Talk About Pioneer Travel

Compare maps with a partner. Compare and contrast the different trails pioneers used. Discuss the obstacles that the pioneers faced on each trail.

Bringing Social Studies Alive

52   **Use with *United States History*, Unit 5**

Plan a Trip to California

Read a Road Map

In the mid-1800s, adventurers from all over the United States and its territories headed for California. They dreamed of striking it rich in the California Gold Rush. Times have changed since then, and so has travel. California is still called "the Golden State," and many people still travel to the state each year. Use a modern highway map to plan your route for a car trip from Chicago to California.

Write an Itinerary

An itinerary is a plan for a trip. Follow these steps to plan an itinerary for a trip from Chicago to San Francisco.

1. Look at a modern U.S. highway map. You may use a road map, an atlas, or a map from the Internet.

2. First plan your route. Think about these questions:

   • What is the most direct route?

   • Which highways are the best?

   • Do you want to make any special stops?

3. Decide how many hours you will travel each day. Assume that you will average about 50 miles an hour. Use the map scale to see how far on the map you can go in one day.

4. Plan time for meals and overnight stays. If you want to do any sightseeing along the way, plan those stops, too.

5. Write your itinerary. Explain what you will do each day. Describe where you will start, how far you will go, and where you will spend the night.

Compare and Contrast

Write a paragraph comparing a trip to California in the 1800s with a modern-day car trip to California.

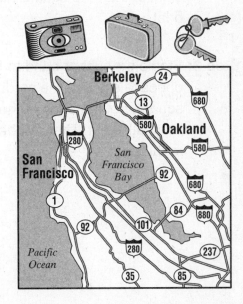

Name _____ Date _____

HANDS ON — **ACTIVITY**

 # Build a Paddlewheel Boat

Introduction

In 1807, a new way of travel was invented—the paddlewheel boat. Make a model paddlewheel boat to see how the paddle moved the boat along. Remember that Robert Fulton's paddlewheel boat was powered by steam. Your boat's power will come from a rubber band.

MATERIALS

- cardboard
- scissors
- rubber band
- stapler
- waterproof paint (optional)

Getting Started

Read the list of materials and gather what you will need. Then look at the diagrams as you follow the steps below to build your model.

Step 1: Cut a piece of cardboard into the shape of a boat's bottom. Make a point on one end. Make the other end square.

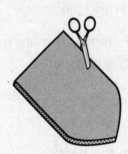

Step 2: Cut a square out of the middle of the boat. Make sure the square comes out in one piece. Trim the sides of the square so it is a little smaller than the square hole in the boat.

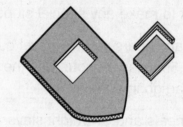

Step 3: Staple the rubber band to two opposite sides of the cardboard square. Let the ends of the rubber band stick out. They will be attached to the boat.

Step 4: Staple the ends of the rubber band to the boat bottom.

Step 5: If you want your boat to last longer, paint it with waterproof paint.

Turn the square backward several times to twist the rubber band. Place your boat in a sink or pan filled with water and watch your boat travel.

Checklist

☐ My model is in the shape of the bottom of a boat.

☐ I used a square piece of carboard for the paddle.

☐ The rubber band makes the paddle turn.

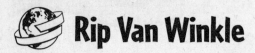

Rip Van Winkle

Until the early 1800s, American culture was linked to Europe. Then Americans began to develop their own culture. One result was a new appreciation for American subjects and authors. One of those authors was Washington Irving. Here is an adaptation of one of Irving's most famous stories.

Cast of Characters

Washington Irving: narrator

Rip Van Winkle: main character

Dame Van Winkle: Rip's wife

Hendrik: young neighbor of Rip

Katje: young neighbor of Rip

Dame Brokaw: neighbor of Rip

Dame Van Buskirk: neighbor of Rip

Strange man

Three bowlers

Man 1

Man 2

Judith: Rip's daughter

The Setting

A village in the Catskill Mountains and the surrounding countryside.

The Props

stick to represent hunting rifle   2 large bundles

ball   fake gray beard

doll

[Rip Van Winkle is leaning against a tree, sleeping. Washington Irving, the narrator, stands to one side.]

Irving: Some say I wrote this story. Some say I made it all up. But I'll tell you the truth. I found this story in the papers of an old man named Knickerbocker. Knickerbocker came from New York, and he liked to write about the descendants of the original Dutch settlers. He wasn't a great writer, but everyone says one thing about him: He was absolutely honest. Everything he wrote was true. Here is one of those true stories.

Dame Van Winkle *(entering):* Rip Van Winkle, why aren't you working? Get up right now. This house is falling down around our ears. Our crops are full of weeds. Your little daughter's ragged clothes are falling right off her back, and your son is getting to be just as lazy as you are. There's not a bit of meat in the house for dinner. Get up and get to work.

Rip *(rising):* What? What? Ah, yes, dear, I was just gathering my strength for a hunting trip. I'm off right now to get us some dinner.

Dame Van Winkle *(exiting):* See that you do! Lazy, good-for-nothing husband!

Hendrik *(entering):* Hey, Van Winkle. We're getting up a ball game! Come join us.

Rip: Not today, Hendrik. My wife says I must go hunting.

Hendrik *(exiting):* Awww! You always play ball with us.

Katje *(entering):* Van Winkle! Van Winkle! Look. My doll broke. Can you fix her?

Rip: Oh, I guess I can take a minute to do that little job for you. *(takes doll and fixes it)*

[Two women enter and stop to smile at Rip and Katje.]

Dame Brokaw: Look at that Rip Van Winkle, Dame Van Buskirk. He is such a good man and always so helpful.

Dame Van Buskirk: Yes, he's always cheerful and ready to help a neighbor. Too bad his wife doesn't appreciate him.

[The two women and Katje exit. Rip walks in place by himself.]

Rip: This should be a good place to hunt. I've never been so high up on the mountain before. What beautiful scenery! But it was a long hike. I need a rest! *(sits and closes his eyes)*

Strange Man *(entering):* Rip Van Winkle! Rip Van Winkle!

Rip *(waking, startled):* Hello, uh, neighbor. You're carrying a heavy load. Would you like some help?

[The two men march off with Rip following behind.]

Rip *(to himself):* What a strange-looking man! His clothes are so old-fashioned.

[Rip, the strange man, and the bowlers pantomime the actions the narrator describes.]

Irving: The two men walked higher and higher up the mountain. Then they stepped into a clearing. There were three bowlers. They, like the man who had brought Rip to this place, were dressed in strange, old-fashioned clothes. The bowlers stopped bowling to stare at Rip. Then the strange man opened his packs and spread out a fine lunch. The bowlers crowded around and motioned for Rip to join them.

The next thing Rip knew, he was waking up. The strange bowlers were nowhere in sight and Rip was back in the spot where he had first met the strange man.

[Rip puts on his beard.]

Rip *(yawning and stretching):* Oh, no! I must have slept here all night. Where did those strange little people go? And what will I tell my wife? I'm in real trouble now. *(picking up his gun)* What's this! My gun is all rusty and broken. How will I hunt? I think those bowlers played a nasty trick on me. I think they took my gun. *(getting up stiffly)* Oh, I'm so stiff. I feel twenty years older. This mountain air must not agree with me. What's this? *(touching his chin)* Where did this long beard come from?

Narrator: With dragging feet, Rip headed home. But when he reached his village, he was in for a surprise. Nothing looked the same, and the people on the streets were strangers. Their clothes looked strange too. Rip headed straight to the store where he and other men in town used to gather to talk. But even the store looked different, and his old friend, storeowner Nicholas Vedder, was not behind the counter. Rip saw a young man sleeping beside a tree and two men in front of the store. He spoke to the men.

Rip: Good day, friends. Maybe you can help me. I'm looking for my old friend Nicholas Vedder.

Man 1: Hello, graybeard. You're a little behind the times. Nicholas Vedder has been dead for eighteen years.

Rip *(gasps):* Nicholas is gone? And what about Rip Van Winkle?

Man 2 *(pointing):* Oh, that's easy. The young good-for-nothing is sleeping beside that tree.

Rip *(to himself):* What has happened? When I went to sleep last night, I knew who I was. Now everything has changed. I'm not even myself.

[Man 1 and Man 2 look at each other knowingly.]

Judith *(entering and stopping to stare):* Who are you, old man? You look just like my father, who disappeared twenty years ago. Ever since then, we've wondered what happened to him.

Rip: I am Rip Van Winkle. I am your father.

Irving: Rip told his story, and Judith took her father home to live with her. Rip learned in amazement about all the things that had happened during his twenty-year sleep. His wife had died. He had missed the whole Revolutionary War and was now a citizen of the United States instead of a subject of the King. Rip lived to a ripe old age. He spent his days on the steps of the store telling and retelling his strange story. Some of the townspeople doubted the story. The writer Knickerbocker, though, swore that the story was absolutely true.

Unit Planner

Long-Term Project Pages 62–63	**Materials Needed**
People in Wartime Mural Students draw scenes for a mural that shows what citizens did during the Civil War. **Time Needed:** 4 weeks **Strand:** Citizenship **Lesson Link:** Chapter 12, Lesson 4 Chapter 13, Lessons 1, 2, and 3	• research materials • research notebook • butcher paper • sketches • chalk • paint or crayons
Geography Activity Pages 64–65	
Sketch a Map Students use a passage to draw a diagram of the third day of the Battle of Gettysburg. **Time Needed:** 30–40 minutes **Strand:** Geography **Lesson Link:** Chapter 13, Lesson 1	• colored pencils or markers
Hands-On Activities Pages 66–67	
Activity 1 **Secret in a Quilt Design** Students make a quilt design that holds a secret map of a place around their school. **Time Needed:** 30–40 minutes **Strand:** Geography **Lesson Link:** Chapter 12, Lesson 2 and 3	• drawing paper • crayons or markers
Activity 2 **Citizens Remember** Students sculpt a memorial of a person or event from the Civil War. **Time Needed:** 30–40 minutes **Strand:** History **Lesson Link:** Chapter 12, Lessons 2 and 3	• clay or various art supplies
Performance Activity Pages 68–71	
The Underground Railroad Students role-play a discussion among people in the 1850s who are considering setting up a new station on the Underground Railroad. **Time Needed:** 30–40 minutes **Strand:** Culture **Lesson Link:** Chapter 12, Lesson 2	none
For Personal Finance, see pp. 108–119.	

People in Wartime Mural

Introduction

In wartime, people have different jobs to do. During the Civil War, Abraham Lincoln's job was to lead the country. Soldiers fought the battles. Other jobs, such as keeping a farm running, were also important. Life goes on during wartime because people do their jobs.

MATERIALS

- research materials
- research notebook
- butcher paper
- sketches
- chalk
- paint or crayons

Project Plan

Week 1: Discuss People's Roles in the Civil War 30 minutes

Call on students to tell about different roles people played during the Civil War. Have students close their eyes and visualize scenes from the Civil War that illustrate the ideas they mentioned. Encourage them to use all their senses to imagine themselves in the scene. Tell students that they will work in groups to draw scenes for a mural that shows what people did during the Civil War.

With students, prepare a chart that lists roles and the people who took them, such as leaders, soldiers (Union and Confederate, from diverse backgrounds), nurses (Clara Barton and others), and people at home (farmers; women running farms and businesses, raising funds, or making bandages). Organize the class into groups and assign one category to each group.

Week 2: Research and Sketch 45 minutes

Have students do research to learn more about the people they will portray on their section of the mural. Suggest that students search for visual representations, such as early photographs by photographers such as Mathew Brady, or paintings. As students do their research, have them notice background details they can use to make the setting historically correct.

Ask students to discuss ways to convey an idea without words through their art. Have students sketch their ideas and use details from each sketch to plan their group's mural drawing.

Week 3: Create the Mural 30 minutes

Tape butcher paper on a wall in the classroom or in the hallway outside the door. Assign one section of the mural to each group. Tell students to use chalk or pencil to transfer details from their sketches to the mural paper. Tell students that pictures for a mural should be large and have simple lines so that the important ideas will stand out when the mural is viewed from a distance. After students are satisfied with their drawings, have them complete the mural by painting or coloring it.

Week 4: Share Ideas 30 minutes

Ask group members to stand beside their section of the mural and have individuals explain the idea behind their drawing to the rest of the class. Suggest that they point out historical details and share information from their research to explain their drawing.

You may wish to invite other classes to view the mural and have students act as guides as they use the mural to summarize important events from the Civil War.

Name _____ Date _____

Sketch a Map

In 1863, after stopping two attacks on Richmond, General Lee marched north into Pennsylvania. The two armies met near the town of Gettysburg.

Make a diagram of the third day of the Battle of Gettysburg.

1. Read the passage below.

2. Draw a diagram of the battle on the map on page 65.

3. Draw or label soldiers in their starting positions. Use arrows and drawings of soldiers to show what the Confederate and Union troops did.

The fighting at Gettysburg began on July 1, 1863, but the biggest battle came two days later. The Union soldiers were on a high ridge above town. It was called Cemetery Ridge. From their camp, they could fire down at any Confederate soldiers who dared to approach.

The Confederate soldiers camped on Seminary Ridge. Cemetery Ridge and Seminary Ridge were about one mile apart. The Union soldiers outnumbered the Confederate soldiers. For two hours, the Confederate soldiers shot nonstop at their enemy. The ground and air around the battlefield trembled.

When the shelling stopped, it became quiet. Then General George Pickett's Confederate soldiers began marching down from Seminary Ridge. The soldiers were brave and calm. They marched in a giant formation. Would this show of force frighten the Union?

The show of force did impress the Union. But the Union soldiers were in the perfect position. From the top of the ridge, they fired at the group of closely-packed soldiers. The Confederate soldiers had no chance. The battle was a turning point of the war.

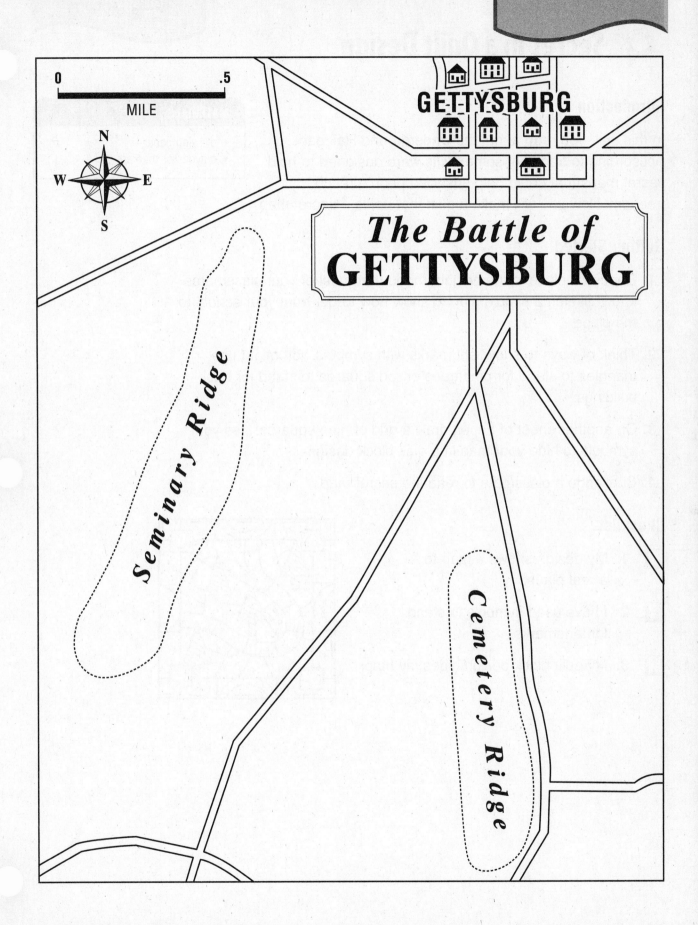

0
.5

MILE

N
W E
S

GETTYSBURG

The Battle of
GETTYSBURG

Seminary Ridge

Cemetery Ridge

Name _____ Date _____

 # Secret in a Quilt Design

Introduction

In this unit, you read about the Underground Railroad. Acccording to tradition, some quilts were designed to hold secret maps that could help enslaved people reach freedom. Now you will make a quilt that holds a secret map.

MATERIALS
- drawing paper
- crayons or markers

Getting Started

1. Choose a place in the neighborhood that most of your classmates know. Sketch a simple map to show how to get from your school to the place.

2. Think of ways to show landmarks with symbols. You might use triangles to stand for pine trees or red squares to stand for brick buildings.

3. On another sheet of paper, draw a grid of nine squares. Use your symbols to hide your map in a quilt block design.

4. Challenge a classmate to read the secret map.

Checklist

☐ **1.** My design shows a map to a real place.

☐ **2.** I have used symbols to stand for landmarks.

☐ **3.** My quilt block design hides my map.

 Citizens Remember

Introduction

The Civil War has been over for a long time, and the United States is united. Many small towns, large cities, and battle sites have statues, or memorials, to ensure that our Civil War heroes will never be forgotten.

MATERIALS
- clay or various art supplies

Getting Started

1. Think about the people and events you read about in this unit.

2. Choose a person or event you especially want to remember.

3. Use clay or other art materials to sculpt a memorial that will help you remember the person or event.

4. Write a few words about the person or event and tape the paper to the base of the statue.

Checklist

☐ 1. My statue shows a person or event from the Civil War.

☐ 2. My statue includes some words of remembrance.

☐ 3. I can explain why it is important to remember the person or event.

The Underground Railroad

Simulation Overview

Tales of the Underground Railroad are an important part of United States culture. In this simulation, students will take the roles of a group of people from the late 1850s who are considering setting up a new station on the Underground Railroad.

Procedures

Review what students have learned about the Underground Railroad.

Then read aloud or distribute the information on page 69. Organize the class into five groups. Give one card to each group and allow time for students to read about their roles and discuss their ideas.

After the groups have discussed their ideas, have students act out the scene. Tell them to stop just before the characters reach their final decision.

At the end of the simulation, have students discuss the pros and cons of becoming an active participant in the Underground Railroad. Have students describe orally or write an ending to each scene to tell about the family's decision.

Overview

Before the Civil War began, the Underground Railroad was established to help enslaved people escape to freedom. The Fugitive Slave Act of 1850 angered many people. Abolitionists and the members of the Underground Railroad worked even harder. But to help as many people as possible, the Underground Railroad needed more workers and more places to hide the fugitives.

You will perform a scene about a family that must decide whether to join the movement and make their home a station on the Underground Railroad. As you act out your scene, remember that secrecy was important. When discussing the Underground Railroad, use terms like *conductor, station,* and *freight* or *packages.* Remember that in this case is it not disrespectful to speak of human beings as *packages* or *freight.* The terms were part of the secret code that protected both enslaved people searching for freedom and the people who helped them on their journey.

- -

Group 1: Adults Who Want to Join

Your family has been asked to join the Underground Railroad. Your home in Oberlin, Ohio, is on a travel route for fleeing enslaved people. If you agree, your house will become a stop, or station. You want to take part. Your home has lots of hiding places. People can also hide in your farm fields. You're not worried about danger. You think you can fool the hunters. In the future, your family will be proud of what it has done.

Good things about this idea:

_____

_____

Possible problems with this idea:

_____

_____

Group 2: Adults Who Are Doubtful About Joining

Your family has been asked to take an active role in the Underground
Railroad. Your home in Oberlin, Ohio, is on a travel route for fleeing
enslaved people. All of you believe in the cause but have doubts about
joining. You know that some neighbors are already helping. You think that
joining is risky. The fugitive-slave hunters are armed and dangerous. The
law is on their side. Your family has always been law-abiding. You think it
is better not to get involved.

Good things about this idea:

_____

_____

Possible problems with this idea:

_____

_____

✂ -

Group 3: Children in the Family

You've heard your parents talking about slavery, but you don't understand
it yet. The decision the family makes will affect you too. It may put you in
danger. If your family joins the Underground Railroad, you will have to
help out. At first, you think the whole thing sounds like fun. You hear words
like *railroad, conductor,* and *freight.* You have lots of questions about the
Underground Railroad. Don't be afraid to ask. The adults will explain.

Good things about this idea:

_____

_____

Possible problems with this idea:

_____

_____

Group 4: Abolitionist Organizers

Some members of your group are white, and some are African American. You have been working together to organize the Underground Railroad all over the country. You want people to join your cause. You're not afraid to speak out about your cause. You can help family members explain slavery, abolition, and the Underground Railroad to the children. You also want to work to convince doubtful adult family members to become part of the Underground Railroad.

Good things about this idea:

_____

_____

Possible problems with this idea:

_____

_____

Group 5: Conductors

You are African Americans who have escaped from slavery. At first, you thought you would never go south again. Then you decided to lead other people to freedom. You've stopped here to find out whether this house will be a safe house on your next trip. You explain that the Underground Railroad needs stations. You tell the stories of some of the formerly enslaved people who rode the Underground Railroad to freedom.

Good things about this idea:

_____

_____

Possible problems with this idea:

_____

_____

Unit Planner

Long-Term Project Pages 74–75	Materials Needed
Local History Book Students research the history of their town and create a class local history book showing how the town has changed over time. **Time Needed:** 4 weeks **Strand:** History **Lesson Link:** Chapter 14, Lesson 2 Chapter 15, Lesson 3	• research notebook • computer with scanner (optional) • construction paper
Geography Activity Pages 76–77	
Sketch a Map Students read a passage about *Little Town on the Prairie* and draw a map based on the description given. **Time Needed:** 30–40 minutes **Strand:** Geography **Lesson Link:** Chapter 14, Lesson 2	none
Hands-On Activities Pages 78–79	
Activity 1 **Make an Invention Expo Poster** Students make posters describing inventions and present them to the class. **Time Needed:** 30–40 minutes **Strand:** History **Lesson Link:** Chapter 14, Lesson 2	• poster paper • markers or crayons
Activity 2 **Build a Sod House** Students work together to build models of sod houses. **Time Needed:** 30–40 minutes **Strand:** Geography **Lesson Link:** Chapter 15, Lesson 1	• strips of paper • clay • craft sticks • dowels or rolling pins • plastic knives
Performance Activity Pages 80–83	
Should We Form a Union? Students role-play a debate about whether to form a union in a local factory. **Time Needed:** 30–45 minutes **Strand:** Economics **Lesson Link:** Chapter 15, Lesson 1	none
For Personal Finance, see pp. 108–119.	

Local History Book

Introduction

In Unit 7, students learn about changes in the Great Plains and in cities. How has your city or town changed through the years? Have students create a class history book to show local changes over time.

MATERIALS

- research notebook
- computer with scanner (optional)
- construction paper

Project Plan

Week 1: Interview Local People 30–45 minutes

Invite students to tell the history of their town. Have them discuss changes that have occurred in their lifetime as well as stories they have heard about the past. Tell students to spend the week interviewing people about local history. Suggest that they talk with older neighbors, friends, and family members—especially those who have lived in the area for a long time. Advise them to take notes about each interview.

Explain that students' goals are to build background that will suggest research topics and to collect information they can use to write a local history book.

Week 2: Plan Research 30 minutes

Call on students to share interesting stories and facts they learned from their interviews. List their data on a three-column chart with the headings People, Places, and Events. Then organize the class into three groups and have each group research one of the categories.

Brainstorm avenues for further research, such as local libraries and historical societies or the Internet. Tell students to find out more about the people, places, or events on their list and to confirm the facts uncovered during their interviews.

Suggest that students also try to obtain photographs. Explain that photos from books usually may not be copied. For photos from individuals, or photos on display in libraries or historical societies, students should ask for permission to copy the photo. If they cannot get permission, suggest that they make a drawing of the person or place in the photo to include in their book.

Week 3: Put It All Together 60 minutes

Have students write a page about each of the historical people, places, or events that they researched. If more than one student researched the same person, place, or event, have them work together to write their page. Have students organize the group's pages in chronological order. Remind students that chronological order is the order in which things happened.

If a computer is available, students may use a word-processing program to write their pages, scan in drawings or permissioned photos, and print several copies of their book. Otherwise, have students edit their drafts, copy them in their best writing, mount their photos or drawings, and assemble the pages between construction-paper covers to make a book.

Week 4: Share Books 30 minutes

Have students read their books aloud and show the pictures. Ask individuals to explain how they found their information and describe any interesting experiences they had. Then have students place their books in the classroom library so other students can read them or check them out to share with their families.

Students may also enjoy making copies of their books to donate to the school and community libraries, or a local historical society.

75   Use with *United States History*, Unit 7

 **Sketch a Map**

An Early Great Plains Town

In the late 1800s, many settlers made new homes on the Great Plains. Some lived on farms. Some built new towns. In *Little Town on the Prairie*, author Laura Ingalls Wilder wrote about the beginning of a small town called De Smet, South Dakota.

Read the passage below. The passage was written by someone who studied maps of De Smet. Use what you read to complete the map on page 77. Draw and label locations on the map.

> In the midst of the farm claims, a small town arose. The settlers named it De Smet. Most of the buildings in town were on Main Street. Charles Ingalls built a store on the southeast corner of Main Street and 2nd Street. The Ingalls family lived in the store in the winters. Most of the other stores were on the other side of Main Street, facing the Ingalls's building.
>
> In the block between 3rd Street and 2nd Street, there were eight building lots. Fuller's Hardware Store was right across from the Ingalls store on the southwest corner of Main and 2nd Streets. Oddly enough, there was another hardware store right across 2nd Street. That was the Couse Hardware Store. The Couse building occupied the first of nine lots in the block between 2nd Street and 1st Street.
>
> The school was set off away from the other buildings. When Laura walked to school, she walked west on 2nd Street and turned right at West Cross Street. The school was about halfway between 2nd and 1st Streets on the west side of West Cross Street.
>
> The Wilder brothers' feed store was on the west side of Main Street. It was the third building from 1st Street. Little did Laura know that she would someday marry Almanzo Wilder.

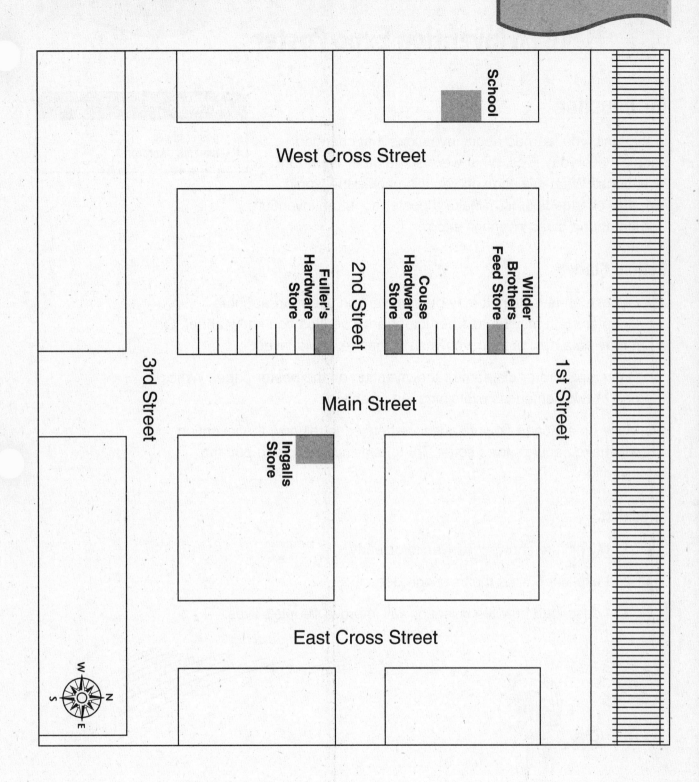

Make an Invention Expo Poster

Introduction

In this unit, you learned about inventions that changed people's everyday lives. What were some other important inventions? What invention do you wish someone would invent to change your life? Make a poster about an invention. Present it at a class invention expo.

MATERIALS
- poster paper
- markers or crayons

Getting Started

1. Choose an invention. It may be an invention you read about in Chapter 15. It may be another important invention you know about. Or it may be a new product you wish someone would invent.

2. Draw a picture or diagram of the invention on the poster paper. Write one or two sentences explaining the invention.

3. Make up a slogan or write a few sentences to tell how the invention will make people's lives better. Try to convince people to buy the invention.

Checklist

☐ 1. My picture shows the invention clearly.

☐ 2. I explained what the invention does.

☐ 3. I described how the invention will improve people's lives.

 # Build a Sod House

Introduction

Settlers who came to the Great Plains from the East were used to building homes with wood. On the Great Plains, however, there were very few trees. The settlers had to use the resources they had and what they had was sod— grass-covered dirt held together by thick roots. They made sod bricks to build homes. Follow the steps below to build a model sod home. Use clay and strips of paper in place of grass, roots, and dirt.

> **MATERIALS**
> - strips of paper
> - clay
> - craft sticks
> - dowels or rolling pins
> - plastic knives

Getting Started

Work in pairs or in small groups.

1. Mix strips of paper with clay. Roll the mixture into a slab. This is your "sod." Cut strips from the slab. Then cut the strips into bricks.

2. Stack the bricks to build a small house. Make sure the structure is tight with no spaces between the blocks. Use craft sticks to build a doorframe and two window frames.

3. Make a roof by laying craft sticks over the tops of the walls. Cover the roof with sod.

Checklist

☐ 1. My structure is sound. There are no spaces between the bricks.

☐ 2. The only wood in my sod home is in the doorframes, window frames, and roof.

☐ 3. The roof is covered with sod.

 # Should We Form a Union?

Simulation Overview

In this simulation, students role-play workers who must decide whether or not to establish a union in a local factory. They will give different points of view.

Procedures

- Distribute the cards and organize the class into four groups. Have each group read about their roles and choose a discussion leader. Allow time for students to prepare their arguments. Suggest that they choose names for their characters and make up a history that explains why they feel as they do.

- After the groups have discussed their positions, begin the meeting. Appoint one of the union organizers to lead the meeting, making sure all sides are heard.

- Some students may come from families who have strong feelings about unions. Explain that for this simulation, participants may need to put aside personal feelings to stay in character. Tell them that one purpose of debate is to understand different points of view.

- At the end of the simulation, have students summarize the pros and cons of belonging to a union. Then have the group vote on whether to unionize their factory.

Overview

The time is the late 1800s. Many people in your area have moved to town to work in a factory. The workers thought they would earn more money. They thought life would be easier. Some workers, however, soon found that their new lives and new jobs did not meet their expectations. The hours were long, and the pay was low. Their families were crowded into small, flimsy apartments. Sometimes their children had to go to work to make ends meet. Meanwhile, factory owners seemed to be making more and more money.

Now a rumor is spreading through the factory. In some places, workers are joining together to form unions. By forming a union, they can improve their lives, but joining a union can be dangerous. It can even be violent.

A group of union organizers has come to town. They want to start a union in your factory. They are having a meeting to explain their ideas. Organizers, workers, and factory owners will all speak. At the end of the meeting, the workers will vote.

Group 1: Union Organizers

You travel around the country organizing unions. You want workers to work shorter hours for better pay. You want factories to be safe. You want the workers to get breaks and time off. You want them to have health care. By working together, union workers can get these benefits.

Some workers are afraid to join unions. Sometimes workers must strike. Sometimes there are fights. If the union loses, the members could lose their jobs. It is your job to convince the workers to join.

Make up a name for your character: _____

Write a sentence about your character: _____

_____

Make notes about things you will say: _____

_____

Group 2: Factory Owners

You feel unappreciated by the factory workers. You take care of your workers. You have given them jobs. They can earn money to buy food and clothes.

They say you should share the wealth, but it was your money that created the factory in the first place. Doesn't the United States Constitution guarantee the right to life, liberty, and the pursuit of happiness? You will not be happy if you have to spend more money. The workers are a bunch of whiners. If they don't like their jobs, they can find new ones.

Make up a name for your character: _____

Write a sentence about your character: _____

_____

Make notes about things you will say: _____

_____

✂ -

Group 3: Pro-Union Workers

You want a better life. From early morning until late at night you are trapped in a dirty, noisy factory. You work six days a week. Some of the jobs are backbreaking and dangerous. A worker could lose an arm in a machine—or worse. You've seen it happen. When it does, the worker is fired. There is no money or insurance to pay doctor bills.

Factory owners have a right to make a profit, but with rights come responsibilities. Workers have the right to be treated fairly. You are on the side of the union organizers. You try to help them convince the other workers to join.

Make up a name for your character: _____

Write a sentence about your character: _____

_____

Make notes about things you will say: _____

_____

Group 4: Anti-Union Workers

You've heard about these newfangled unions. They make lots of promises, but they stir up trouble. You've read about strikes. All the workers refuse to work, and the owners lose money. Sometimes strikes work, but sometimes they turn violent.

There is more to lose than to gain by joining a union. You have a job now, and you could lose it. You have a roof over your head—even if your home is crowded and shabby. You can avoid being hurt on the job if you're careful.

Make up a name for your character: _____

Write a sentence about your character: _____

_____

Make notes about things you will say: _____

_____

Discussion

Fill out the chart to summarize the discussion.

Joining a Union

Pros	Cons

Take a vote. Only the workers may vote for or against the union.

Unit Planner

Long-Term Project Pages 86–87	**Materials Needed**
To Market, To Market Students learn about the stock market by "buying" shares in a real company and tracking their investments. **Time Needed:** 4 weeks **Strand:** Economics **Lesson Link:** Chapter 16, Lesson 4	• research notebook • newspapers or Internet access
Geography Activities Pages 88–89	
Activity 1 **A Man, a Plan, a Canal—Panama** Students learn how the Panama Canal makes sailing between the Atlantic and Pacific Oceans faster and easier. **Time Needed:** 30–40 minutes **Strand:** Geography **Lesson Link:** Chapter 16, Lesson 1	• outline map of the Western Hemisphere • ruler • string
Activity 2 **Draw Maps to Show Change** Students make maps that show how a real or imaginary city looked before and after World War II. **Time Needed:** 30–40 minutes **Strand:** Geography **Lesson Link:** Chapter 16, Lessons 2 and 5	• prewar maps or atlases from a library or historical society (optional) • modern maps or atlases (optional)
Hands-On Activities Pages 90–91	

Activity 1 **Hawaii Diorama**
 	
Students make a diorama of Hawaii's resources.
 	
Time Needed: 30–40 minutes   **Strand:** Economics
 	
Lesson Link: Chapter 16, Lesson 1
	• Internet access • crayons or
	  or reference paint
	  materials • scissors
	• empty shoebox • paste or glue
	• art materials

Activity 2 **Home Front Soldiers** Students pretend to be living during one of the World Wars and make posters to encourage Americans at home to work and sacrifice to help the war effort. **Time Needed:** 30–40 minutes **Strand:** Citizenship **Lesson Link:** Chapter 16, Lessons 2 and 5	• poster board • paints • found art materials
Performance Activity Pages 92–95	
A Historic March Students put on a play about the 1963 civil rights march in Washington, D.C. **Time Needed:** 30–40 minutes **Strand:** History **Lesson Link:** Chapter 17, Lesson 3	none
For Personal Finance, see pp. 108–119.	

 # To Market, To Market

Introduction

Send students to market—the stock market, that is—to learn how stocks work and why the stock market crash of 1929 was a major cause of the Great Depression.

Project Plan

Week 1: Research Stocks 45 minutes

Have students reread Chapter 16, Lesson 4. Summarize by saying that in times of prosperity, many people have extra money to invest. One way to invest is by buying stock. Explain that the value of stock can change every day. It can grow quickly. It can also lose its value quickly. Until investors sell their stock, they cannot really know how much money they will gain or lose.

Tell students about today's stock market. Investors can buy stock in most major companies and many smaller ones. The difficult part is knowing which stock to buy. Some financial advisors suggest that beginning investors buy stock in a company whose products or services they use themselves.

Tell students to spend the week making a list of companies whose stock they think might be a good investment.

Week 2: Choose Stocks to Buy 30–45 minutes

Have students name the companies on their list. Write each company name on the chalkboard and make a tally mark beside the name for each student who listed it.

Organize the class into five groups. Assign one of the five most popular stocks from the list to each group. Tell each group that they will "buy" 100 shares of their stock and track the stock's progress. In two weeks, they will sell their stock to see whether their investment earned or lost money.

Explain that each company has a special symbol for its stock. Model how to find the symbol on the Internet and use it to see how much the stock is worth. Have each group find the worth of one share of their stock and multiply it by 100 to see how much they will "invest." Have them write the date and amount of their investment in their notebooks.

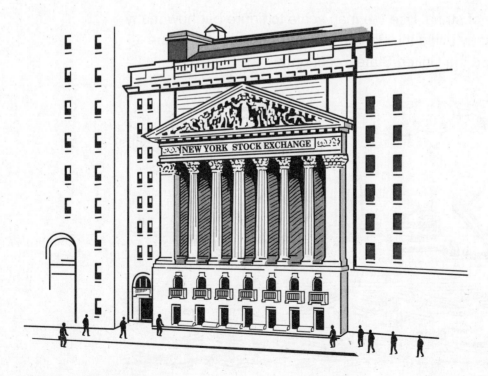

Week 3: Track Stocks 30–45 minutes

Have each group use newspapers or the Internet to find out how the price of their stock has fluctuated during the week since they "bought" it. Have them figure out how much money they would gain or lose if they sold the stock immediately.

Tell students to look for news stories that might explain major changes in the price of their stock and record the information in their research notebooks.

Week 4: Cash In 30–45 minutes

Tell students that today is the day they will "sell" their stock and record their profit or loss. Have each group find the current price of one share of their stock and multiply the price by 100 to see how much money their stock is now worth. Then have them refer to their research notebooks to find out how much they paid for their 100 shares of stock.

Tell them to subtract the number that represents the cost of the stock when they bought it from the number that represents the price of the stock today. If the number is a positive number, it stands for a profit. If the number is a negative number, it stands for a loss.

Call on each group to tell how much they earned or lost. Ask them to share news stories about the stock market in general or about the company they chose that might explain why the price of their company's stock rose or fell.

NEW YORK STOCK EXCHANGE

A Man, a Plan, a Canal–Panama

Before 1914, people who wanted to sail from a city on the Atlantic Ocean to a city on the Pacific Ocean had to sail all the way around the southern tip of South America. President Theodore Roosevelt had a better plan. He had a canal built across the isthmus of Panama. When the canal was completed in 1914, ships were able to cut many miles and days from the long journey. Learn how the Panama Canal made sailing between the Atlantic and Pacific Oceans faster and easier.

MATERIALS

- outline map of the Western Hemisphere
- ruler
- string

Map Shipping Routes

1. Locate and mark New York City, NY, and San Francisco, CA, on your map.

2. Draw a line to show the shipping route between the two cities before the Panama Canal was built.

3. Draw another line to show the shipping route between the two cities after the Panama Canal was completed.

4. Use string to measure the length of each route.

Compare Shipping Routes

Measure each piece of string. Use the map scale to figure out how many miles shippers saved by using the Panama Canal. Talk about how the Panama Canal helped the United States' economy.

Name _____ Date _____

Draw Maps to Show Change

Before World War II, many people lived in cities surrounded by fields, forests, small towns, and farms. When the war ended, the soldiers came home. They were ready to settle down, and they needed homes. There was not enough room in the cities, so the new families built new homes in suburbs. Suburbs created a new way of life.

MATERIALS

- prewar maps or atlases from a library or historical society (optional)
- modern maps or atlases (optional)

Make City Maps

Make two maps. For the first map, show an imaginary city as it looked before World War II. Use a bird's-eye view to show a business area in the heart of the city and neighborhoods with small stores and homes. Show the area around the city too. If you have a map or atlas that was published before World War II, you may refer to it to draw a map of a real city instead of an imaginary city.

Draw a second map of the same real or imaginary city and its surroundings. Show how the area looked after suburbs were built. If you drew a real city, refer to a modern map or atlas.

Discuss Change

Compare your maps. Talk about changes the new suburbs caused. How did transportation change? What happened to cities? How did building new homes affect the ecology? What happened to school systems?

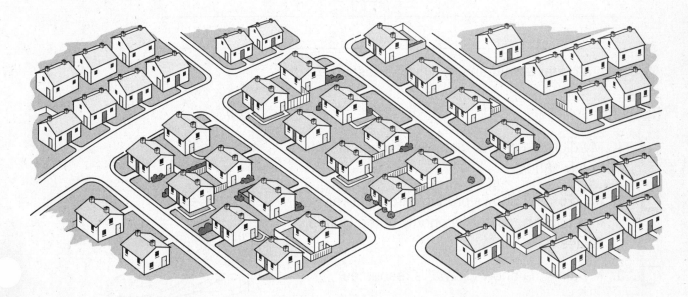

Bringing Social Studies Alive

Use with *United States History,* **Unit 8**

Name _____ Date _____

Hawaii Diorama

Introduction

In this unit, you have read how the United States grew in size. Now you will show why Hawaii should become part of the United States by making a diorama of its resources.

MATERIALS

- Internet access or reference materials
- empty shoebox
- art materials
- crayons or paint
- scissors
- paste or glue

Getting Started

You are an American planter in Hawaii in the 1800s. You want to show that owning Hawaii would be beneficial to the United States.

1. Read about Hawaii in your textbook. Use other sources for information about Hawaii in the 1800s.

2. List Hawaii's positive features. Include products that could boost the economy of the United States.

_____

_____

_____

_____

_____

_____

_____

3. Make a diorama that shows Hawaii's resources.

Checklist

☐ **1.** My diorama shows that I researched Hawaii in the 1800s.

☐ **2.** My diorama shows products from Hawaii that could boost the economy of the United States.

☐ **3.** My diorama shows Hawaii's resources.

Bringing Social Studies Alive

Use with *United States History*, Unit 8

 # Home Front Soldiers

Introduction

Americans worked together during World Wars I and II. Soldiers fought overseas. People at home helped the war effort too. Imagine that the president has asked you to design a poster to encourage Americans at home to work and sacrifice to help the war effort.

Getting Started

1. Think about things Americans at home did to help win World War I and World War II. Use your textbook and other sources for ideas. List your ideas.

_____

_____

_____

_____

_____

2. Choose one job and design a poster to tell about it. Write a slogan to explain what the job is. Draw a picture to make your idea clear. Make your poster colorful to attract attention.

Checklist

☐ 1. My idea is clear and easy to understand.

☐ 2. My poster is colorful and has a picture that attracts viewers' attention.

☐ 3. My poster includes a slogan that helps people remember my main idea.

Bringing Social Studies Alive

Use with *United States History*, Unit 8

A Historic March

The civil rights movement began in the 1950s. By the 1960s, it was in full swing. To encourage political support, African American leaders, including Dr. Martin Luther King, Jr., organized a peaceful march on Washington. The leaders hoped for a large group of supporters, but they never expected the crowd of over 200,000 people who participated in the demonstration.

Cast of Characters

Adult George:	narrator
Young George:	same character, as a 10-year-old boy
Jody:	George's sister, a 12-year-old girl
Mom:	George and Jody's mother
Dad:	George and Jody's father
Sandy:	12-year-old girl
Jimmy:	10-year-old boy
Dr. Martin Luther King, Jr.	

Scene 1: A family living room in the 1960s

[Adult George, the narrator, stands to one side. Mom, Dad, Young George, and Jody are seated center stage facing each other.]

Adult George: It's been more than forty years now since that hot day in August when my family and I joined the March on Washington. It meant so much to me, as an American who values justice and equality, to hear Martin Luther King, Jr., speak. It was a long time ago, but it seems like just yesterday. Here's how it all began.

Dad: You know, I've been hearing more and more about this March on Washington that Dr. King is planning. It makes me think.

Jody: Me too, Dad. We've been talking about it in school every day.

Young George: March on Washington? What's that?

Mom: It's a demonstration, George—a peaceful demonstration. There's a law before Congress that could end segregation forever. Dr. King wants Congress to know how many people support that law.

Dad: I've been thinking that this family should join that march.

Jody: Oh, yes! Can we? But won't it cost a lot to travel to Washington, D.C.?

Dad: Where there's a will, there's a way. I've heard that some people are getting together to charter special buses. It will be good to be with other people who want to end segregation. And we can pack food to eat along the way.

Mom: I'm still not sure. The cause is just, and the march is supposed to be nonviolent. But you never can tell. People have been hurt over civil rights.

Dad: It's important to support things that you believe in.

Mom: Yes. I want my children to grow up in a country in which everyone is treated equally.

Young George: Me too, Mom!

Dad: The march might be dangerous, but it will also be wonderful. And I think that it's important for our family to be there. Some things are worth the risk.

Jody and George: We think so too!

Scene 2: Near the reflecting pool in front of the Lincoln Monument in Washington, D.C.

[The narrator, Adult George, stands at one side of the stage. Dr. King stands at the other. Mom and Dad stand behind Jody and Young George, who are seated on the ground at the edge of the pool.]

Adult George: So that settled it. Jody and I started counting the days. Mom still seemed a little nervous, but we could tell she was getting excited too. The big day finally came. We boarded the bus expectantly. As we got closer to Washington, we grew more and more amazed. Buses and cars were everywhere. We'd known there would be lots of people at the march. We didn't find out until later that there would be more than 200,000 people. Luckily, we were able to find a place near the reflecting pool. No one was in front of us. We'd be able to see everything!

[Sandy enters with Jimmy right behind her and sits down beside George.]

Sandy: Wow! What a great place to sit!

[Jimmy waves toward the distance to signal their parents, while Sandy smiles at George and Judy.]

Sandy: Hi, I'm Sandy, and this is my brother, Jimmy. Would you like to share some of our grapes? Our parents are still squeezing through the crowd.

Jody: Sure, and please help yourselves to a sandwich. We've got plenty.

[Jimmy sits down.]

Jimmy: Where are you folks from?

Jody *[smiling at Jimmy and Sandy]:* We're from North Carolina. We had a long bus ride to get here. Where are you from?

Jimmy: We're from Iowa.

Young George: Iowa! That's really a long trip. I guess people are coming from all over the country.

Sandy: We were in the car for 3 days, but I'm glad we made the trip.

[The four kids smile at each other.]

Mom: Kids, look! That's Dr. King. He helped to organize this march because he knows that segregation has to stop. He knows that getting the law changed will be difficult, but he's brought us all together to continue the fight.

Dad: That's right. He has inspired us all to work for equality for all people.

Young George: We will, Dad. I know we will.

Adult George: So that's how it was on that long-ago day in August. I'll never forget the day I became part of history. I don't think anyone else who was there will forget it either.

The End

Unit Planner

Long-Term Project Pages 98–99	Materials Needed
Land of Many Cultures Students research different ethnic groups in the United States. **Time Needed:** 4 weeks **Strand:** Culture **Lesson Link:** Chapter 19, Lesson 2	• research notebook • resource materials • presentation materials
Geography Activity Pages 100–101	
North American Neighbors Students draw a diagram to show how the United States, Canada, and Mexico are similar and different. **Time Needed:** 30–40 minutes **Strand:** Geography **Lesson Link:** Chapter 19, Lesson 1	none
Hands-On Activities Pages 102–103	
Activity 1 **Run for Office** Students create a poster and write a short campaign speech for a political office. **Time Needed:** 30–40 minutes **Strand:** Citizenship **Lesson Link:** Chapter 19, Lesson 3	• poster board • markers
Activity 2 **Citizens Volunteer** Students make volunteer activity cards of ways that they can help their community. **Time Needed:** 30–40 minutes **Strand:** Citizenship **Lesson Link:** Chapter 19, Lesson 3	• large note cards • card file
Performance Activity Pages 104–107	
Citizens Pay Taxes Students role-play citizen groups and council members in a town meeting on what to do with surplus tax money. **Time Needed:** 30–40 minutes **Strand:** Economics **Lesson Link:** Chapter 19, Lesson 3	none
For Personal Finance, see pp. 108–119.	

 # Land of Many Cultures

Introduction

Compared to some countries, the United States is very young. As a country, it has had to develop its own traditions. Many traditions that have become part of American culture were brought to the United States by immigrants from other countries. Students will research an ethnic group and create a presentation about the contributions the group has made to the United States.

Project Plan

Week 1: Discuss Cultural Diversity 30 minutes

Remind students that ethnic groups are groups of people who share a common heritage. People who belong to the same ethnic group often have ancestors who lived in the same country. They may share a language and many traditions. Explain that the population of the United States includes people of many different ethnic groups. Each ethnic group has added traditions to United States culture.

Ask students to name ethnic groups they have heard about. List the groups that students name on chart paper. Save the list.

Tell students that they will research an ethnic group and make a presentation about how the ethnic group contributed to the United States culture.

Week 2: Research an Ethnic Group 30–45 minutes

Reread the list of ethnic groups, and ask students to add the names of other groups they may have learned about in the past week. Then divide the class into teams that will research the ethnic groups.

Have each team research their ethnic group's language, food, music, arts and crafts, and customs and holidays.

Week 3: Plan the Presentation 30–45 minutes

Allow time for the teams to meet and to share information they learned as they researched. Tell the teams to appoint a recorder to track the research data and presentation ideas.

Have students work together to decide which information they will share and how they will divide the presentation tasks. Prompt students by suggesting that they play ethnic music, share recipes for ethnic foods, and explain traditions and holidays. Tell students to create visual aids to share during their presentation.

Week 4: Make a Presentation 60 minutes

Have each team give its presentation to the rest of the class.

Summarize the presentations by displaying a world map on a bulletin board. Have students write about or draw pictures to show how each ethnic group contributed to United States culture. Have students attach their writing and pictures to the bulletin board and use strips of yarn to connect each contribution to the country in which it originated.

Name _____ Date _____

 # North American Neighbors

The United States shares the continent of North America with two close neighbors. Those neighbors are Canada and Mexico. Both countries share some characteristics with the United States. Each country is unique in many ways too.

Compare and Contrast

Follow these steps to compare and contrast North American countries.

1. Look at the maps of Canada and Mexico in Lesson 1 and at the North American Landforms map on page 7 of your textbook.

2. Review Lesson 1 to find the similarities and differences between the United States and its two neighbors.

3. Use the Venn diagram. List characteristics that are unique to each country in the circle below the country's name.

4. Next, list characteristics that Canada and the United States share in the space where the circles overlap.

5. Now, list characteristics that Mexico and the United States share in the space where the circles overlap.

Share Conclusions

With a small group, discuss the three North American countries.
Use notes from your organizer to help you share information.

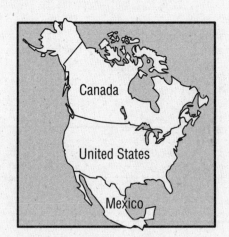

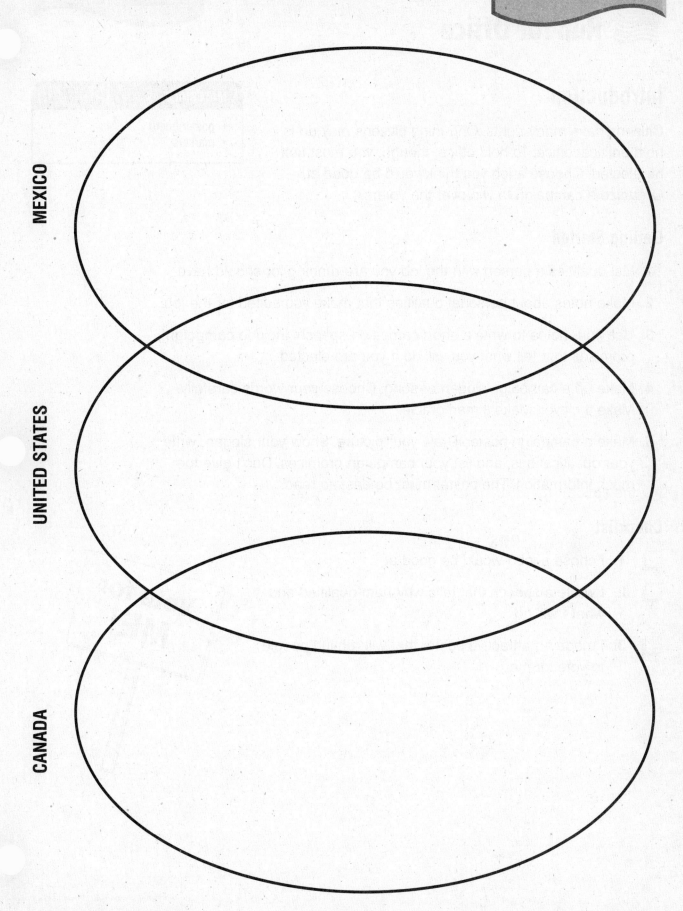

MEXICO

UNITED STATES

CANADA

HANDS ON **ACTIVITY**

 **Run for Office**

Introduction

Citizens have many rights. One thing citizens may do is hold political office. To hold office, though, you must first be elected. Choose a job you think you'd be good at. Organize a campaign to win over the voters.

MATERIALS
- poster board
- markers

Getting Started

1. List qualities a person with the job you are running for should have.

2. Make notes about personal qualities that make you suited for the job.

3. Use your notes to write a short campaign speech. Include campaign promises that tell what you will do if you are elected.

4. Make up a campaign slogan or song. Choose your words carefully. Make it clever. Make it memorable.

5. Make a campaign poster. Draw your picture. Show your slogan, write your qualifications, and list your campaign promises. Don't give too much information. The poster must be easy to read.

Checklist

☐ 1. I chose a job I would be good at.

☐ 2. I wrote a speech that tells why I am qualified and what I will do.

☐ 3. I made an attractive poster that will remind people to vote for me.

Vote for ME!

HANDS ON ACTIVITY

 **Citizens Volunteer**

Introduction

MATERIALS
• large note cards
• card file

Some citizenship activities, such as running for city, state, or federal office, can only be done by adults. People of any age can work to make the community better, though. One way is to be a volunteer. A volunteer helps other people without being paid. Make some volunteer activity cards to give your classmates ideas of ways they can volunteer.

Getting Started

1. Think about ways students your age can volunteer to help out at school, in the neighborhood, or with a community organization.

2. Choose three activities and write about them on large note cards.

3. Start by writing a title for the activity. Then tell where and when people can perform the activity. If volunteers need special skills or talents, list them on the card.

4. Place your card in the class volunteer activity file.

Checklist

☐ 1. I have written about activities students can do in different places.

☐ 2. I have included important information about each volunteer activity.

☐ 3. I have added my activity cards to the class volunteer activity file.

 **Citizens Pay Taxes**

Simulation Overview

In this simulation, students will take the roles of council members and citizens as they participate in a town meeting to decide how surplus tax money should be spent.

Procedures

Discuss what students have learned about citizens' rights and responsibilities. Remind students that citizens are responsible for paying taxes. It is the government's responsibility to use those taxes to pay for services citizens want or need.

Read aloud the information below. Then distribute the cut-out cards and organize the class into five groups. Give one card to each group and allow time for students to read about their roles and discuss their ideas.

After the groups have discussed their ideas, call on the Council President to begin the meeting.

At the end of the simulation, have students from the council member group vote on how to spend the surplus funds. Have all council members explain why they voted as they did.

Overview

Taxes for this year have been collected, and your town has had a nice surprise. People paid more taxes than were expected. Your small town has a surplus of $50,000. It is up to the town council to decide what to do with the surplus. Of course the citizens have a right to express their opinions. Citizens will speak about the matter at the town council meeting. The council members will listen to the citizens' ideas. At the end of the meeting, the council members will vote to decide what to do with the money.

Group 1: Town Council

You ran for election, and the voters chose you. They expect you to be a leader. They trust you to do the right thing. But each voter seems to have a different idea about what the right thing is. You want to do what is best for your town. You want to carry out the will of the people. You also want to be reelected for another term in office.

Each council member will help run the meeting. Assign these roles to group members.

Council President: Your job is to chair the meeting. You begin by calling on the treasurer. You call on different speakers and make sure every citizen has the opportunity to talk. You must make sure no one takes too much time or is rude to another speaker. At the end of the meeting, you ask the secretary to read back the citizens' ideas. Then you call on council members to cast their vote out loud.

Council Treasurer: You are in charge of the town's money. You are the person who discovered the surplus. When the president calls on you, you tell how much extra money the town has. You explain where it came from.

Council Secretary: You take notes during the meeting. As citizens offer their ideas about ways to spend the surplus money, you write the ideas on the board. At the end of the meeting, you tally the votes for each idea.

Council Members: You listen carefully to each speaker. You may ask the speaker questions. You must answer questions the citizens ask you. At the end of the meeting you will vote for one of the citizens' ideas.

Bringing Social Studies Alive
105

Group 2: Build a Community Pool

Your town doesn't have many activities for families and students. You think the town needs a swimming pool. The surplus money will make a good down payment for a pool. Each group member will speak at the meeting. You will try to convince the council members to spend the money for a pool.

Write notes for your speech:

_____

_____

_____

_____

✂ -

Group 3: Save for an Emergency

Your town may have some extra money right now, but you can remember when there was too little money, not too much. You are sure hard times will come again. When they do, you want your town to be prepared. You think the council should vote to save or invest the money. Then it will be there whenever it is needed for an emergency.

Write notes for your speech:

_____

_____

_____

_____

         Use with *United States History*, Unit 9

Group 4: Lower Taxes

If the town has more money than it needs, it's because it collected too much money in the first place. You think taxes are much too high. After paying taxes, a person has much less money to spend. You think the council should include the money in next year's budget. Then the town won't need to collect so much money, and next year's taxes can be lower.

Write notes for your speech:

_____

_____

_____

_____

Group 5: Fix Up What We Have

You think there are many old things that need to be fixed up. Some roads have potholes. They should be repaved. The town should replace old traffic signals and streetlights. You want the council members to take care of what the town has before spending money to get something new.

Write notes for your speech:

_____

_____

_____

_____

A Family Budget

Tell students that it is important for families to understand their monthly budget. Ask students to give examples of items that cost their family money every month (for example, groceries, electricity, gas, cable TV, rent or house payment, and so on).

Read aloud and distribute the following introduction.

> The Esparza family has a computer that is old and slow. The children have asked for a new computer. However, after all the bills are paid, there's no money left over to buy a new computer. What can they do?
>
> The family's monthly budget is $2,000. That's the total amount of money they have to spend each month. The family decides to start saving $200 every month by cutting back on their spending. In a few months, they hope to have saved enough money to buy a new computer.
>
> How can you help the Esparza family save $200 each month?

Have students study the monthly budget of the Esparza family on page 109. Then ask students to imagine helping the family to save money for a new computer. Direct them to write each budget item next to their ideas for saving money, the amount they think they could save, and the new monthly cost. Point out that their monthly savings should total $200.

A Family Budget

Here is the Esparza family's monthly budget. Suppose the Esparzas decide to set aside $200 every month so that they can save for a new computer. Study their family budget below. Then start making changes to it.

1. For each Budget Item in column 1, write a way for the family to save money in column 3, How to Save Money. There may be some items that cannot be cut.

2. Write how much they could save for each Budget Item under Savings, in column 4. If you do not think they can save money on an item, write $0.

3. Write the new cost for each Budget Item under New Cost, in column 5. The New Cost should be Today's Cost minus the Savings.

Esparza Family's Monthly Budget

1. Budget Item	2. Today's Cost	3. How to Save Money	4. Savings	5. New Cost
Food from grocery store	$400	*Clip newspaper coupons*	$10	$390
Eating out	$100			
Housing	$700			
Entertainment	$100			
Clothing	$200			
Transportation (gas, bus fare)	$200			
Electric, gas, phone	$300			
TOTAL	**$2,000**		**$200**	**$1,800**

Balancing a Checking Account

You can put money that you earn or receive into a checking account. You can take cash out of your checking account. You also reduce the amount of money in your checking account when you pay for something with a check.

You write on the check the name of the company or person you are paying, the amount you are paying, and the date. You give or send the check to the person. When the company or person gives your check to their own bank, the money comes out of your checking account and goes to the company or person.

How would you keep track of how much money you had in a checking account? The bank gives you a **check register** to help you. Each time that you put money in or take money out, you can write the amount, or **transaction**, in the check register. Here are the headings in a check register.

- Check #: What was the number of the check?

- Date: When did the transaction take place?

- Transaction Description: What was the transaction? If you wrote a check, to whom or what store did you write it?

- Check Amount: If taking money out, for how much was the check?

- Deposit: If putting money in, how much was it?

- Balance: How much money is in the checking account after the transaction is finished?

Your **balance** is a record of how much money you have in the account. When you take out money, subtract the check amount from the last balance. When you deposit money, you add the deposit amount to the balance.

Taking Money Out	New Balance = Last Balance – Check Amount
Putting money in	New Balance = Last Balance + Deposit

Suppose that you have your own checking account. Fill in your check register with the next four transactions:

1. On March 20, you use check #1711 to pay $5.00 for a movie ticket at Star Theater.

2. The next day, you buy lunch at City Diner with check #1712 for $3.99.

3. On April 7, you put a $200 paycheck into your account.

4. You use the next check to donate $10 to the Town Animal Shelter on April 1.

Your Check Register

Check #	Date	Transaction Description	Check Amount	Deposit	Balance
1709	2/24	Sun Market Groceries	$85.19		$539.32
84534	3/7	Paycheck		$200.00	$739.32
1710	3/14	Circle Store T-shirt	$16.25		$723.07

Be sure to write down the correct information for each transaction, including the balance.

Learning Means Earning

Why should you go to school? There are many important reasons. One of those reasons is that your financial future may depend on it. On average, in the United States, people who stay in school longer make more money than those who do not. The chart below shows how the amount of schooling affected the earning power of five people.

People	School	Yearly Salary
Drew	Dropped out of high school	$ 10,839
Heidi	Graduated with a high school diploma	$ 18,571
Colleen	Went to college for a while but didn't finish	$ 20,998
Ashley	Earned a two-year associate's college degree	$ 26,536
Banji	Earned a four-year bachelor's college degree	$ 40,387

The amount of schooling you have can increase the amount of money you can earn in the future. Some jobs ask for people who graduated from high school; others ask for people with a college degree. The chart below shows a list of jobs and how much schooling is required for each job. You can also see the average salary a person starting each job can make in one year.

Job	School	Yearly Salary
Accountant	4-year college degree	$34,500
Chemical Engineer	4-year college degree	$46,900
FBI Agent	4-year college degree	$34,400
Flight Attendant	High school diploma	$13,700
Travel Agent	High school diploma	$13,770

Name _____ Date _____

For each of the three people below, write down which jobs they
could have. Use information from the chart on page 112. Keep in mind
that the people who went to college also graduated from high school.

People	Job Options
Banji	Accountant
	_____
	_____
	_____
	_____
	_____
Heidi	_____
	_____
	_____
	_____
	_____
	_____
Drew	_____
	_____
	_____
	_____
	_____
	_____

Which person has the most job options? _____

113

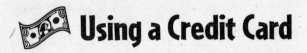

Using a Credit Card

Tell students that when a person uses a credit card to pay for something, he or she is borrowing money from the bank that issued the card. The borrower must pay the bank back. If the borrower pays back everything he or she owes in the first month, the bank will not charge interest. If the borrower pays only part of what is owed, the bank will charge interest. (Interest is a percentage of the amount owed, which a borrower pays the bank in return for getting the loan.) The bank also asks the borrower to pay at least a minimum amount toward the debt every month. The longer it takes to pay back the amount owed, the more it will cost the borrower.

To demonstrate the cost of credit to students, give them the following examples.

- Larvell uses his credit card to buy $200.00 worth of clothes and shoes. His interest rate is 20%. He pays $10.00 per month toward this debt. It takes him about two years to pay it off. After interest, his $200.00 purchase ends up costing him about $245.00.

- The Taylors use a credit card to pay for repairs to their family car. The repairs cost $475.00. The minimum payment is $10.00 per month, but they are able to pay $50.00 each month. It will still take the Taylors 11 months to pay back the money. And at 16% interest, it will cost them about $510.00 by the time they finish.

- Candace uses her credit card to buy a $900 computer. Her interest rate is 18%. She can only afford to pay the minimum payment, which is $20 per month. It will take Candace over six years to pay off her debt, and it will cost $1,500.00!

Bringing Social Studies Alive

114

Use with *United States History*

Borrowing Using a Credit Card

Describe the following scenarios to students. For each scenario, ask students to guess how long it will take to pay off the debt and how much they think it will cost. Then tell them the real answers and discuss each scenario as a class.

1. The Schneiders go to a family reunion in another state. Their expenses add up to $500.00, which they charge to their credit card. The interest rate on their card is 10%. They pay $50 per month. How long will it take them to pay off the debt? How much will it cost?
   (11 months/$525.00)

2. Joaquin uses his credit card to pay a $300.00 hospital bill. The interest rate on his card is 20%. He pays $20.00 each month. How long will it take him to pay off the debt? How much will it cost?
   (17 months/$350.00)

3. Marlina's refrigerator stops working. She uses her credit card to buy a new one that costs $800.00. The interest rate on her card is 10%. She can pay $25.00 per month. How long will it take her to pay off the debt? How much will it cost?
   (37 months/$935.00)

Ask students to draw some conclusions about using credit cards and taking many months to pay the debt.

 **Investing**

When you invest your money, you do so with the hope that you will earn more money. For example, you can buy U.S. savings bonds. After a period of time, you can cash them in for more than you paid for them. Here are some ways to invest money.

Investment Type	Positive Points	Negative Points
Bank Saving Account	You can withdraw your money at any time. Your money is safe. There is almost no risk.	You do not earn very much interest on your money.
Bank Certificates of Deposit (CDs)	You can earn more money over a period of time than with a regular savings account. Your money is safe, and your risk is low.	You cannot withdraw your money whenever you want. You must wait, usually for a period of at least six months.
U.S. Savings Bonds	The money you are lending to your country helps the country. Your money is safe, and your risk is low.	Some bonds do not increase in value very much.
Stock Market	If your stocks do well, you can earn a great deal of money very quickly.	Your risk is very high. If your stocks don't do well, you can lose money in the stock market.
Collectibles	You may be able to sell collectible objects, such as rare coins, for more than you spent on them.	Your risk is very high. You can get your money back only if you find a buyer willing to pay the price.

Imagine that Uncle Bob has given you $5,000.00 to invest for the future. Look at the chart on page 116 to help you decide how to invest the money. If you want to, you can invest the money in more than one way. On the lines below, write a letter to Uncle Bob explaining how you intend to invest the money and why.

Dear Uncle Bob,

_____

_____

_____

_____

_____

_____

_____

_____

_____

_____

_____

_____

_____

_____

_____

_____

Sincerely,

_____

 # Advertising

Businesses advertise to try to get people to buy their products or services. Examples of advertisements are television commercials, ads in newspapers and magazines, flyers, and brochures.

A product that is advertised may be of the same quality, better quality, or worse quality than a similar product that is not advertised. It may be the same price, more expensive, or less expensive than a similar product that is not advertised.

Some companies use "appeals in their advertisements.

Appeal	Description	Example
Testimonial	Uses a popular person to promote a product	"If the number one quarterback uses Mighty-White toothpaste, shouldn't you?"
Repetition	Repeats a product or company name numerous times to help you remember it	"Furniture City is at it again! Furniture City is throwing their annual Furniture City Super-Sale. Come to see us at Furniture City."
Bandwagon	Gives the impression that most people are using this product	"Three out of four people surveyed loved the new taste of Bubbarama Bubble Gum."
Glittering Generalities	Makes something sound amazing or "cool" without telling much about it	"Hip-Pop Jeans: Rocking the Hood."
Urgency	Persuades you to buy something quickly	"Act now! Supplies are limited!"
Emotional Language	Stirs up your emotions	"Don't you hate the way your bank treats you? Don't you deserve better than that?"
Something for Nothing	Convinces you that you'll be getting a free bonus	"And that's not all! We'll also include a set of kitchen knives absolutely free with every order."

Read the advertisement below carefully. Then list what appeals
the company is using in this ad to persuade people to buy the product.
Remember that sometimes more than one appeal may be used at the
same time. Be sure to include examples for each answer.

Example Ad

Fusion

America's Favorite Purple Hand Lotion

Fusion is here.

Fusion is now.

Fusion is you.

Are you tired of rough, dry hands? Are you afraid to
show them to your friends? Do you wish you could have
smooth, silky hands like everyone else? Fusion Hand
Lotion is the answer.

"I couldn't make it through the day without my Fusion,"
says actress Clara Shonash. "Why wouldn't I use it?"

Order four bottles of Fusion before July 31 and take
advantage of our free shipping offer.

Appeals

Appeal	Example

Answer Key

Unit 1

Page 4: Lots of Water . . . Can You Drink It?

3. Water covers about three-fourths, or 75 percent, of the earth's surface. Students' calculations may fall between 65 and 80 percent due to map distortion and counting or tracing errors.

Bar Graph Student graphs should reflect accurate proportions.

Students should conclude that in proportion to the total water on Earth, there is very little fresh drinking water available.

Page 5: Many Regions, One Map

1–2. Students' maps should include a unique key for each American Indian nation. Maps should reflect American Indian regions as given in the textbook.

3. Paragraphs will vary. Students should recognize that neighboring nations had the greatest opportunity to trade with one another.

Page 6: Make a Model of an Artifact

Check to see that the artifact is appropriate to the American Indian group chosen.

Page 7: Build an Anasazi Village Model

Student models should reflect the following: clay was used for walls; houses had few windows; some houses were built into the sides of cliffs.

Unit 2

Page 16: Where Are We Going?

1–3. Check that students have marked the most likely route from where they live to the region targeted on the globe.

4. Check students' destination and travel plans.

Page 17: What's in a Name?

1. Shaded area should include the areas shown on the textbook page 111: Mexico, Arizona, California, Nevada, most of New Mexico and Texas, Utah, parts of Colorado.

2. Rio Grande River.

3. Check that students locate El Paso, Texas, where the boundary of New Mexico meets the Rio Grande River.

4. The river moved quickly and unpredictably; the valley had a warm, moderately wet climate.

Page 18: Post-Expedition Wrap-Up

3. Check that students' presentation accurately reflect the climate, landforms, plants, and animals encountered during the chosen expedition.

4. Suggestions for moneymaking enterprises will vary but should be appropriate to the regions explored. Items such as furs and cash crops might be proposed. All natural resources available for possible commercial use should be mentioned. Students should recognize that land was both a natural resource and a political resource of the time.

Page 19: Classroom Compact

2. Student responses for rights and responsibilities will vary. Sample answers:

	rights	responsibilities
classroom	safe, quiet	clean, orderly, listen to speaker
school	clean, effective education	attend regularly, complete assignments
neighborhood	safe passage to and from home, street lights, crossing guards	report problems to authorities

3. Students' test case should be able to be resolved with listed rights and responsibilities. Moderate proceedings so that classroom compact reflects realistic rights and responsibilities.

Unit 3

Page 28: Produce a Product Map

3. Maps may vary; however, students should develop legends for crops and industries as follows. **New England Colonies** crops and animals: wheat, oats, peas; industries: shipbuilding, fishing, whaling. **Middle Colonies** crops and animals: wheat, corn, barley, cattle, pigs; cash crops: wheat, corn, cattle, pigs. **Southern Colonies** crops and animals: various; cash crops: tobacco, rice, indigo, pitch.

4. Check students' maps to ensure they have placed resources correctly and that all the symbols are in the legend.

Page 29: Settlement Patterns

1. slanted stripes

2. Grey

3. Fall line should be about 150 miles inland from coast.

4. Black

5. Pennsylvania, North Carolina

6. English

7. Answers will vary. Sample answer: People who wanted to be free of religious persecution tended to settle along the frontier. Also, these settlers could be sure of having farmland for crops and woods for hunting. The disadvantages of settling far from populated areas include loneliness and lack of help in case of emergency.

Page 30: Trading Cod for Cloth

Check students' maps to ensure that they have drawn a triangular trade route and that they show the following exports. Colonies: lumber, cod, other foods. West Indies: molasses and sugar. England: teas, spices, and manufactured goods.

Page 31: Wish You Were Here!

Student handbills will vary. Check to ensure that handbills include required items. Dutch handbills might stress trading opportunities, Puritan and Quaker handbills might stress religious freedom, English handbills from Virginia might stress prosperity.

Unit 4

Page 38–39: Create Cartoons About Taxes

Presentations should include a brief explanation of the tax and its purpose. Student cartoons should include a tax officer or collector as well as a colonist and an illustration of the tax. The **Staple Act of 1663** required that the goods enumerated in the 1660 act be shipped exclusively to England where they would then be re-exported giving a greater profit to English merchants. The **Molasses Act of 1733** set a high tariff on molasses brought into the colonies from non-British locations. The **Stamp Act of 1765** required colonists to purchase stamps from royal tax collectors for a variety of items, including legal documents, playing cards, newspapers, and land titles. The Stamp Act was repealed in 1766. The **Townshend Act of 1767** imposed duties on glass, paint, lead, paper, and tea imported into the colonies. In 1770, the Townshend duties were repealed except for duty on tea. **The Tea Act of 1773** granted the East India Company a virtual monopoly over the British tea market by placing the cost so low that even with the tea tax, East India Company (British) tea was less expensive than Dutch tea.

Page 40: Saratoga Battle Plan

Check students' maps to ensure that they used different symbols for planned and actual troop movements. Check that maps correctly depict battle plans and actual troop movements.

Answer Key *continued*

Page 41: Blockade!

1. Answers will vary. Students' lists should indicate a variety of transportation and communication routes serving their community.

2. Answers will vary. Sketches are likely to show that ground transportation would be the easiest to block, followed by air transportation. Students might recognize that blocking communication is likely to be most difficult.

3. Check to ensure that students' lists of affected goods and services are compatible with listed blockade routes.

4. Answers will vary. Accept any answers that students can justify.

Page 42: Make a Diorama

Check students' lists to ensure that they accurately list battle conditions. Student dioramas should identify the battle depicted, illustrate three details about the battle, and use at least three different materials.

Page 43: Make a Primary Source Artifact

Students' amendments should illustrate an accurately worded amendment in the Bill of Rights. Each student amendment should have at least two features that indicate it is an official document: visual aids, such as drawings or public domain photographs of the President, maps, graphs, or charts.

Unit 5
Page 52: Traveling West

Check students' maps for accuracy of placement of landform features and placement of exploration trails.

Page 53: Plan a Trip to California

5. Itineraries will vary but should include what students will do each day, where they will start, how far they will go, and where they will spend the night.

   Compare and contrast paragraphs will vary but should contain comparisons between the ease of travel today and the difficulties and dangers associated with travel in the past.

Unit 6
Page 65: Sketch a Map

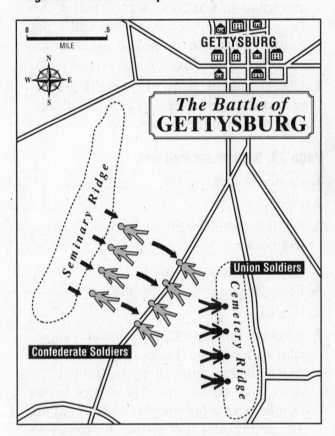

Page 66: Secret in a Quilt Design

Quilt patterns will vary. The patterns should show a design using symbols to hide a map.

Unit 7

Page 77: Sketch a Map from a Passage

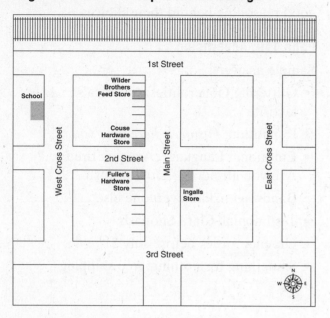

Unit 8

Page 89: A Man, a Plan, a Canal—Panama

Students should draw two lines from New York to San Francisco. One line should go around the southern tip of South America. The other should go through the isthmus of Panama in Central America.

Answers will vary. Students should figure out that the Panama Canal cut approximately 11,000 miles from the trip between New York and San Francisco.

Unit 9

Page 101: North American Neighbors

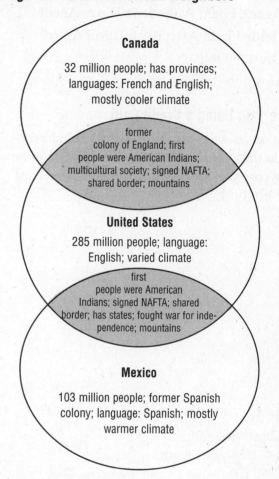

Personal Finance

Page 109: A Family Budget

Answers will vary, but Savings should total $200 and New Cost should total $1,800.

Page 111: Balancing a Checking Account

Check # 1711; Date: 3/20; Description: Star Theatre, Movie ticket; Amount: $5.00; Balance: $718.07

Check # 1712; Date: 3/21; Description: City Diner, Lunch; Amount: $3.99; Balance: $714.08

Check # 85426; Date: 4/7; Description: Paycheck; Amount: $200.00; Balance: $914.08

Check # 1713; Date: 4/11; Description: Town Animal Shelter, Charity; Amount: $10.00; Balance: $904.08

Answer Key *continued*

Page 113: Learning Means Earning
- Banji: Accountant, Chemical Engineer, FBI Agent, Flight Attendant, Travel Agent
- Heidi: Flight Attendant, Travel Agent
- Drew: NONE
- Most job options: Banji

Page 115: Using a Credit Card
Responses will vary, but students should conclude that taking many months to pay can be very costly, especially if the debt and interest rate are both high.

Page 117: Investing
Answers will vary, but students should provide good reasoning behind their choices.

Page 119: Advertising
Sample answers:
- Glittering Generalities; America's favorite . . .
- Repetition; *Fusion is here/now/you*
- Emotional Language; Are you tired . . .? Are you afraid . . .? Do you wish . . .?
- Bandwagon; like everyone else
- Testimonial; Clara Shonash
- Urgency; order before July 31
- Something for nothing; free shipping